WRITING THE SCRIPT

WRITING
THE SCRIPT

A Practical Guide for Films and Television

WELLS ROOT

An Owl Book

Holt, Rinehart and Winston

New York

First published in January 1980 by Holt, Rinehart and Winston, 383 Madison Avenue, New York, New York 10017.

Published simultaneously in Canada by Holt, Rinehart and
Winston of Canada, Limited.

Library of Congress Cataloging in Publication Data

Root, Wells.
    Writing the script.
    Includes index.
    1. Moving-picture authorship.   2. Television
authorship.   I. Title.
PN1996.R67   808.2'2   79-1927
ISBN Hardbound: 0-03-044226-5
ISBN Paperback: 0-03-044221-4

Designer: Robert Bull
Printed in the United States of America
10 9 8 7 6 5 4

In Loving Memory of
MIMI

Contents

Preface

This book combines thirty years of professional writing experience with a thousand nights of teaching film and television writing at the University of California at Los Angeles.

The UCLA Extension course offers professional approaches to screenwriting to a wildly mixed bag of non-professionals. I have taught junior high students and Ph.D.'s; actors, doctors, lawyers, housewives, businessmen and business women, reporters, secretaries, construction workers, chicken ranchers, and a famous New York detective; browns, blacks, and Orientals.

Many of these students have asked me to put our discussions on paper. Especially, some who have become professionals seek a permanent reference and promptbook. These chapters are a grateful memoir for them, and for apprentices and practicing craftsmen everywhere.

Our discussions deal primarily with technique and craftsmanship. Fundamentals like Original Stories (they don't exist), How to Get an Agent, Conflict, Suspense, Theme and Content, and the two deep foundation stones, Emotion and Characterization.

But I must warn newcomers and cynics alike to read every chapter and every verse with dark distrust, just as I warn my students, in the dictum of George Bernard Shaw: "The unbreakable rule of playwriting is that there is no unbreakable rule."

Then why write a book—or give a course—in chaos? Because writing for the theater or screen is a craft that respects odds and percentages. Certain techniques devised by the ancient Greeks work miracles at your neighborhood movie theater. Others are disastrous. There are filmmakers, such as Bergman, Altman, Fellini, and Kubrick, who have riddled the old rules with irreverent—often wildly successful—invention.

But today's mass audiences for film are not the classic Greeks or the intellectual elite of New York and Europe. They are mankind itself. If you are going to convince or convulse that worldwide jury, you had best write as Shakespeare did—for the pit. The world's great dramatists have always done so, from the ancients to the Elizabethans to Molière, Eugene O'Neill, and Noël Coward. So do such present American champions of screen, stage, and TV as Paddy Chayefsky and Neil Simon.

Only the proven work of master craftsmen can sustain a practical study such as this. Because success in the theater—be it writing, directing, or acting—depends on attracting an audience. Without that audience, a script is a reading experience, or an exercise for actors facing an empty house. Without a very costly production to attract that audience, the finest screenplay ever written is a stapled stack of wastepaper.

What persuades producers to launch that production to attract that audience? This book attempts to analyze, in audience terms, those higher odds and percentages, those basic writing themes and techniques that work—and some that don't. By reference to plays and films of great craftsmen, we focus on the bottom line of an ancient trade. That has always been the line outside the box office buying tickets.

Let us go directly to the critical question. I have seen it mirrored in the questioning eyes of a hundred starting classes:

What are my chances of becoming a professional film or TV writer?

Great writers bring their gifts with them at birth. Just as Chris Evert and Pete Rose were born with the timing to hit the impossible smash. But talent comes in small, medium, and luxury sizes. Thousands of players, lacking the magic of Evert or Rose, draw professional pay. I have found that many people with a true urge to write have creative abilities.

You need more than that, however. You need the combining skills and the sweat glands required to put a screenplay together. A writer must be an engineer and a midwife. He must know how people dream, as well as how they die. He must know how fast or how slow to drive the train. And he must know when to smash it up.

"Talent is helpful in writing," Jessamyn West once said, "but guts are an absolute necessity."

Let us say that you have the two essentials—a gleam of natural talent and a compulsion to write that forbids doubt. What can this book offer you?

The answer is technique and craftsmanship. Talent without technique crawls on its knees through the marketplace.

There are absolutely vital elements to be learned about how to write film and TV scripts. And even more to learn about how *not* to write them. An ultimate technique may lie in learning what to leave out. But most of the positive knacks of film writing can be analyzed and passed along. That is the aim and function of this book. Technique and craftsmanship are simply plush words for know-how.

Our studies will show you how to use mortar and stone to build a lighthouse—to paraphrase a thoughtful adage—"but the light that shines from it must be your own."

ACKNOWLEDGMENTS

Nelson Gidding pressed the switch that sparked this book's publication. William Abrahams guided its development. Burt and Adele Styler and Laura Levine shared with me invaluable insights in their special field of comedy. Mike Kaplan, editor of *Variety*'s forthcoming *International Encyclopedia of Show Business*, tapped the myriad resources of that reference work for facts, figures, notes, and functional memorabilia. Michael Dewell lent significant aid with the final editing.

There remains my greatest obligation—to my over twelve hundred students at UCLA Extension. In truth, this book was written for them in our weekly meetings over many years. Whatever resides in these pages that film and TV writers need to know, I owe to that abundant experience.

WRITING THE SCRIPT

1.

TELL ME A STORY

The Beginning, the Middle, and the End

The design of most film and TV scripts goes back thousands of years to nights before film or formal theater ever existed. Vagabond storytellers brought their ballads and magic legends to campfires and castle courtyards. In caves and jungle huts sleepy children murmured:

"Tell me a story."

Film and TV audiences are still the eternal children. If you seek to make a living writing scripts for them, your practical first step is to master the three-act design.

It's often called in Hollywood *the beginning, the middle, and the end.* We will draw a full diagram in a few moments, specify basic ingredients, and explain how you put them together.

But let's break the ice with a well-known descriptive summary credited to George M. Cohan, the only seven-threat man in American theatrical history: star dramatic artist, director, producer, writer, lyricist, composer, and song-and-dance man.

Cohan summed up the beginning, the middle, and the end this way:

"In the First Act get your man up a tree." By "your man" he meant the central character, your hero. By "up a tree" he meant confront him with a dramatic problem or crisis.

"In the Second Act throw stones at him." By "throwing stones" he meant intensify your man's problem: almost stone him off his perch.

"In the Third Act get him down out of the tree." By which Cohan meant, resolve your man's crisis or problem.

His summary has a small problem of its own. It is too neat. Students tend to question it as irreverent, and not covering all the bases. What about three-hour movies like *Doctor Zhivago?** What about Shakespeare's five-act plays? What about half-hour situation comedies like "All in the Family" and "M*A*S*H"?

Even though Cohan had never seen a half-hour situation comedy, or *Doctor Zhivago*, he knew what he was talking about. His summary covers them all.

Confusion lies in the word *act* and what it means to you. In the theater acts are division points where the curtain falls to let the audience go out and buy a drink. In television, acts fade out to give the sponsor air time to sell shoes, ships, or sealing wax. But when we discuss acts we are talking about the three essential stages in the structure of most films and television dramas. Here is a picture of those three steps.

* Screen authorship credits for *Doctor Zhivago* and all film and TV scripts named in this book are listed in "Who Wrote the Script?"—a special writers' index section, page 192 and following.

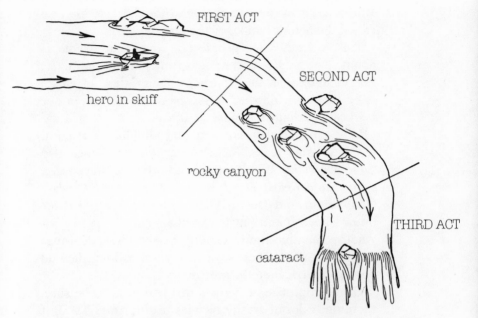

FIRST ACT

hero in skiff

SECOND ACT

rocky canyon

THIRD ACT

cataract

First Act. Diagram represents a rocky, tumbling river. In this first act you launch your hero and/or heroine in a frail skiff. Once on the way, there is no turning back.

Second Act. The river angles sharply, since your audience should never see ahead, or you will lose suspense. Rocks and rapids make safe passage for the flimsy skiff apparently impossible.

Third Act. Again the river angles sharply. Dead ahead is a roaring cataract. If your protagonist goes over the brink he is bound for glory. How you resolve that final crisis we will explore presently.

First Act

Your first act, in most dramatic stories, serves four essential functions:

1. Introduction of the star character (or characters)—also called the hero (heroine) or the protagonist.

This is vital, since people are what your drama is about. Not gats and gimmicks, but human character. So substantial is this character factor that an entire later chapter is devoted to it, one of the longest in our book and perhaps the most significant.

Most great stories center on an individual. But not a few have dual leads. *Romeo and Juliet* was one. Also *Gone with the Wind.* More recently we have seen *Bonnie and Clyde*, *The King and I*, *Midnight Cowboy* (Jon Voight and Dustin Hoffman), *The Turning Point* (Anne Bancroft and Shirley MacLaine).

2. Another notable figure usually makes his appearance in your first act. That is the heavy, the villain, the bad guy, formally called the antagonist.

Never minimize or belittle this bad guy. To be sure, there are a lot of trashy heavies in films and TV. But remember the great ones: Rod Steiger in *In the Heat of the Night*, Judith Anderson as Mrs. Danvers in *Rebecca*, to say nothing of Shylock in *The Merchant of Venice* and the great white shark in *Jaws*.

Your villain is all-important in several respects. It is his job—someone has said—to drive the action toward catastrophe. Actors love to play the part because it may be the most colorful in the cast. For writers villains are a joy to create. You can explore all those awful pits inside you, and then denounce them with touching piety.

3. The third essential of your first act is to shake up your audience with a disturbance, a problem, or a crisis. Why?

Why must your play open with your protagonist facing a crisis? The question I'm most often asked by people outside the film business is: Why do films have to trade on violence, sex, illness (the doctor series), terror, or tension? The answer is primary. People don't reveal themselves under placid conditions.

You and I are covering up most of our waking life. Observe a gambler playing poker. He is forced to bluff, to mask his aces—or lack of them. So must we all much of the time.

Audiences go to the movies or watch TV to see characters blow their cover. Drama puts people under a microscope called a plot. Plot is a succession of crises which rip loose those masks.

That is why dramatic writing has been called the *art of crisis*. And that is just where you usually open your script—in crisis. More about that—much more—in Chapter 6, "Beginning Your Screenplay."

4. The fourth element to establish in your first act is the *or-else factor*. Also called, pedantically, the *dreadful alternative*. That means, simply, the fate in store for your hero if he does *not* solve his plot problem. Examples:

In *Jaws*, will the hero kill the shark, or be eaten alive?

In *The Towering Inferno*, will the folks get out of the skyscraper, or be burned to death?

In *The Goodbye Girl*, and many other love stories, will male and female split up or decide to do it always? Bet on always.

This or-else factor is essential to charge the drama with apprehension, expectancy, *suspense*. In television, if you don't have suspense, there is a still more dreadful alternative (for the network). The viewer may switch to another channel.

Second Act

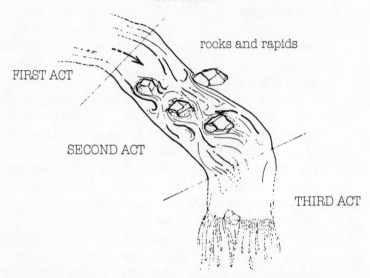

Reviewing our design diagram, we find that the second act is a wicked stretch of river, boiling with rapids, studded with rocks. Our hero, in his flimsy skiff, faced treacherous water in the first act, but this is ridiculous. He can't possibly get through alive.

These rapids and these rocks are the author's devices to intensify the hero's problems. They suggest that things are going to get a lot worse for him before they get better. They are called the *complications*.

His boat scrapes the first rock, and he loses his oars. Swirling free, he rams the second rock, and the skiff springs an ominous leak. Crashing into the third and biggest rock, our hero is tossed into the water. The torrent sweeps him around the last bend, in sight of the cataract. At this point we discover that he cannot swim!

This is his hour of truth, the point of no return. It's called the climax. In a tragic story he goes over the cataract. In an affirmative ending, you, the author, fish him out of the river and up on dry land.

This middle section of river, this canyon of complications, is usually the long stretch of your story. In a half-hour TV show you may only have time for one or two complications. In an hour episode of a weekly series you can devise more rocky smash-ups—which means a more intricately crafted plot. In marathon movies like *Doctor Zhivago* or *The Godfather*, complications interbreed and multiply for ninety minutes or more— until you reach the cataract of no return.

Complications is a stuffy, indigestible word. Let's vitalize it with examples from film and classic fiction. We will start with a movie called *Deliverance*, a modest success in the season of 1972. We are choosing *Deliverance* because its plot is an uncanny mirror image of our three-act design diagram.

A vacationing party of city dwellers, male, start down a remote mountain river on a raft. The river is rock-studded, swift, and dangerous. They survive near-fatal mishaps until the middle of the second act, when two spooky natives attack them from the forest. Massive complication. In reprisal and self-defense, our city crew kills one of the natives. Now they discover that the dead man is a known local character. The redneck sheriff will not dismiss lightly his violent death at the hands of city strangers. Our crew has passed the point of no return. The cataract ahead of them is a murder charge or a lynching.

This plot line is so strikingly similar to our design pattern that an automatic assumption arises. We lifted it.

But we didn't. This river diagram was devised for our class a dozen years before *Deliverance* was produced. Furthermore, the *Deliverance* script was based on the novel by James Dickey. I'm sure that Dickey never heard of TV Workshop X 453 at UCLA Extension. It was just one of those weird cases of coincidental conception.

Back to exploring complications by example. In most love stories the pits on the pathway of love are the complications. In *The Sound of Music*, Julie Andrews, an innocent nursemaid from a convent, falls in love with her rich employer, Christopher Plummer. She discovers that he is engaged to a glossy baroness. Anguished complication.

In *Close Encounters of the Third Kind*, hero Richard Dreyfuss strives to verify the active existence of flying saucers. His problem is sorely complicated by the U.S. Air Force's determination to stop him. He rides down those roadblocks and makes it anyway.

In *All the President's Men*, the two reporters seek to disentangle the Watergate burglary. The complications are the constant frustrations thrown in their way by most of Washington, including the White House itself, and their own newspaper. They succeed regardless.

In our old friend *Cinderella*, the gentle heroine is forced to flee the ball before the sexy Prince has even asked her name. She lands back in the family kitchen, scraping the garbage and scrubbing the floor. But now her problems are complicated by a broken heart.

Thus your second act thrives on complications to a dramatic problem. They multiply and mount until the protagonist is swept into the third act. Now he must finally succeed or fail, win love or lose it, survive or perish.

Third Act

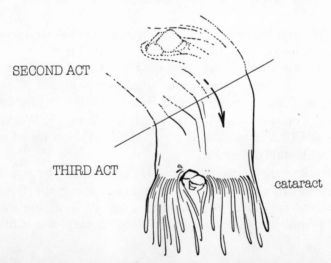

SECOND ACT

THIRD ACT

cataract

If you are writing the third act of a tragedy, your protagonist goes over the cataract. Great tragic stories rank among the masterworks of dramatic writing. But such themes are rare in the common experience. They demand the highest levels of creative concept and achievement. Moreover, from the practical point of view, they raise investment resistance.

Investors are sentimentalists. About money. From the moment a small fortune is born, they nurture it zealously. They learn quickly that affirmative—or at least constructive—endings return highest dollar profits. A random list would include: *Star Wars*, *The Poseidon Adventure*, *The Sting*, *Rocky*, *The Sound of Music*, *The Graduate*, *The Towering Inferno*, *American Graffiti*, *My Fair Lady*, *Close Encounters of the Third Kind*, and *Jaws*. Their profits have run into hundreds of millions.

These matters are analyzed in greater depth in Chapter 7, "Ending a Dramatic Story." For the moment let's accept the undisputed box-office verdict that mass audiences prefer winning over losing. This suggests that a professional writer had better know how to rescue his hero from the cataract and get him back up on dry land.

How, indeed?

You employ an item of equipment found in every playwright's workbox. It is invisible, but it has a stubborn breaking strength. Call it the *life line*.

Check back for a moment to our master design diagram. Add a character to the sketch—yourself. You, the author, are shadowing your hero down the bank of the unruly stream. Over your shoulder you are carrying this coil of invisible rope. When he is about to be swept over the cataract, you throw him the rope.

What coil of rope? Where the hell did it come from?

You ought to know. It came from somewhere back in the first or second act. You planted it there yourself.

The simplest example I can give you comes from fiction's standby, the murder mystery. The life line in a Columbo, Sherlock Holmes, or Kojak story is the hidden clue or unexpected twist that the detective produces at the finish to convict the murderer.

But your writer's life line is not just a mechanical gim-mick of smart policemen. It runs through all of romantic and much of dramatic storytelling. Mark Twain used it early in *A Connecticut Yankee in King Arthur's Court*. Remember, our Yankee hero was about to be burned at the stake. He proph-esied that the day he died the sun would black out and King Arthur's kingdom would be destroyed. The eclipse of the sun was his life line. When it started, King Arthur panicked and set the Yankee free to become his master magician.

In *Jaws* the life line was the dynamite that blew up the shark. In many action-adventure stories it is some special skill or act of heroism that enables the good guys to wipe out the bad. In the classic western it is the marshal's ability to draw faster than the deadly outlaw.

But the ladies resort to it, too. Shakespeare used it to get Portia out of terrible third-act trouble. Remember, in *The Merchant of Venice*, how Shylock was about to extract the pound of flesh nearest Antonio's heart for an unpaid debt? He had the right to do it, too, by written contract. But Portia, in her legal sagacity, discovered a forgotten Venetian law that voided con-tracts which threatened a citizen's life. That pulled Antonio back up on land.

Surely the most famous life line in classic storytelling is the glass slipper. Remember how Cinderella had apparently lost the Prince forever? Until he arrived at her humble cottage with the glass slipper she'd lost fleeing from the ball? It fit her tiny foot, and they are still living happily in the ever after.

This life line, therefore, is whatever device you can use to resolve your hero or heroine's problem. Many great life lines include a bonus of grateful surprise. The audience gets an electric shock. Viewers exchange looks that say: "Why, of course!"

But the technique has certain strict limitations. It must be logical. Not cloud-built or contrived. It should not be just wild luck, such as a lightning bolt killing the heavy or a flash flood drowning all the escaping bandits.

Your life line should not be a *deus ex machina*. That is Latin for "a god from the machine." In ancient Greek or Roman theaters, when a bumbling playwright had third-act trouble, he brought a god or goddess down on a rope from on high (hidden platforms). The god was all-knowing, all-powerful, and he simply solved the hero's problem for him. That was just too easy, and became a classic no-no. It's been modernized something like this:

Don't let bad luck or the good God wipe out the heavy. Your hero must do it!

For those who like to document diagrams with notes, the three-act design sifts down to this:

First Act (Beginning)	Second Act (Middle)	Third Act (End)
1. Introduce your star character(s).	Intensify your hero's problem with complications.	Resolve his problem, affirmatively or tragically.
2. Face him with a problem or crisis.		
3. Introduce his antagonist (the bad guy).		
4. Set up the *or-else factor*, or *dreadful alternative*.		

Postscript

Remember Shaw's unbreakable rule. For this and all following chapters there is no unbreakable rule.

This three-act design principle is never a rigid structure. It is a generalized framework, elastic and flexible. Almost every great story you can think of will reveal striking variations. Originality lies in creative distinctions. The beginning, the middle, and the end is a concept to start with. Where you go with it is a measure of your creative imagination.

In fact, a number of filmmakers, critics, and intellectuals reject the three-act design. Flatly. Indignantly. They say, among other things, that the tidy, packaged quality of the beginning, the middle, and the end is superficial. It is too patent a manufacture. In life things never happen that way.

Indeed they don't. "No one has ever seen," said Picasso, "a natural work of art." In any field of art, ancient or modern.

In films you start with a concept. You develop it in any manner within your reach and competence. No divine rulebook limits any writer, or director, or producer's game plan. Bergman, Resnais, Antonioni, Kubrick, Fellini, Altman, Cassavetes have as much right to freeborn story flights as Disney has to fantasyland.

The one thing the writer and director must do is to communicate with an audience. Without that audience to watch, listen, applaud, be inspired, or perhaps throw eggs, you have nothing but shadows dancing in an empty barn. *How* you communicate is nobody's business but your own. But you had damn well better do it in a fashion that will summon bodies to the barn.

Ultramodern, unstructured story design has an erratic record for bringing bodies to the barn. It is even condemned as nonstorytelling—aimless, confusing, and self-indulgent. Modern landmark films have emerged, nevertheless, such as *Hiroshima Mon Amour*, *L'Avventura*, *Last Year at Marienbad*, and *8½*, and many more.

For such films and their makers, there is a devoted audience. Perhaps not in the multimillions, but in loyal and sufficient numbers to sustain their dreams. With the vivid addition of a box-office smash now and then, like Kubrick's *2001: A Space Odyssey*.

Radical technique films are as essential to our industry's progress as research is to medicine. They represent the experimental labs where adventurous minds are seeking new dramatic dimension. Allow me to simplify it totally. D. W. Griffith (*The Birth of a Nation*) was one of the earliest experimenters. In those bygone days, camera angles were almost exclusively medium or longer shots. Working with his cameraman, Billy Bitzer, Griffith, that wild-eyed radical, conventionalized a startling technique. He called it a *close-up*.

Techniques of today's modernists will seem equally commonplace fifty years from now. By 2030 new radicals will have appeared who will patronize Resnais, Fellini, and our avant-garde as stuffy conservatives.

In the long view, story structure has some kinship to building a house. Architectural inventions in this century have been wild and inspiring. But houses that people will pay for and inhabit still must provide shelter, light, privacy, and facilities for heat and water. The basics.

Worldwide audiences demand corresponding basics in storytelling. Since the craft arose thousands of years ago, listeners have been absorbed by a Prince and a dragon. The dragon captures the Princess. The Prince slays the dragon, and lays the Princess. The audience goes home enchanted.

If that be primitive, make the most of it. The structure of *Star Wars* and thousands of the favorite stories, plays, and films of the ages are—in their essentials—just that primitive. Often the primitive in an art becomes the perennial.

2.

CHARACTERIZATION

Playing God. Making People.

Playwrights make people. That is the beginning and the basic end of playwriting. Characterize. Create people.

But how?

How do you fashion living beings out of the ink trails across a barren of white paper? William Archer, critic, playwright, and author of a once-standard text on writing plays, said morosely: "There are no rules for creating character, any more than there are rules for growing six feet tall."

This widely quoted concept has a clear defect: it is just not true. If there is no specific recipe for character drawing—like Julia Child describing how to jelly eels—there are certainly practical guidelines. We will examine nine of these in a few moments. But first let's consider the relationship between characterization and the vehicle in which the characters are traveling—the plot.

The plot of most movies compares with the steel framework of a rising skyscraper. It holds everything together. Incidents in a film cannot happen simply at random. When they do, the audience just sits there confused. To be sure, in some wildly modern screenplays, things do simply happen at random. Which illustrates the point: audiences sit there confused.

When the skyscraper is finished, the street people can't see the steel frame inside, and many don't realize that it is there. Equally, audiences may not be conscious of the plot because they are so engrossed in the film. Yet without the steel framework the building would collapse in a heap, and so would most film and TV dramas.

Who designs this inner plot framework?

The writer, of course!

No. Wrong! In thousands of fine films the leading character, your protagonist, is the architect. This protagonist *does what he does* throughout the story *because of what he is*. Your plot is his character in action.

We will illustrate by an exalted example. Best loved and revered of all fact or fiction in our Western culture is the saga of Christ. He was the protagonist.

He set Himself the inconceivably difficult task of persuading men that He was the Messiah. He performed miracles; He preached treason; He made converts. His preaching, converts, and miracles aroused deadly antagonists, men corrupted by power. In the end, they crucified Him.

The plot of that ageless drama was fashioned by Christ Himself. The events expressed His *character*—call it Divinity if you will—*in action*. He did what He did because of what He believed Himself to be—the Son of God.

Since art is nonpartisan, we will offer equal time to the opposition. *The Godfather Part II* is the devil's testament, one of the highest moneymakers in theater history. The protagonist is a Mafia *capo*. He finally sacrifices even his wife and children to maintain his diabolic power. The plot is a case history of his character. He does what he does because of what he is—an evil genius.

With a comedy, we complete the triad. George Bernard Shaw's *Pygmalion* was a legend in the theater. Set to music as *My Fair Lady*, it broke stage and screen box-office records. The story pits Professor Higgins, an omnivorous intellectual, against an ignorant flower girl, Liza Doolittle. The plot substance in all versions is the fiery conflict of the characters.

Selection of three classics should not suggest that character dominates plot only in masterpieces. Let's examine, in some detail, a good film that is not well known in America. We'll take *Scent of a Woman*, a tragicomedy made in Italy, starring Vittorio Gassman. The plot materials, however unusual, were well within the range of perceptive writers. Although an effective film, it did not attract mass audiences on Main Street, probably because it was a "foreign" product, with Italian dialogue.

Gassman plays an army colonel, blinded in the line of duty. He is so hostile and embittered by his blindness that he is almost a social savage. He insults and humiliates everybody he talks to, including a young, idealistic army corporal assigned to him for a vacation trip from Milan to Naples. But the colonel is violently attracted to women; he can smell them across a hotel lobby or a street in Rome. Hence the title. He busies himself mostly with prostitutes.

At the end of their trip, in Naples, lives a girl who loves him. She's the daughter of another officer, also blinded in the line of duty. She has loved our colonel since she was a child, with an adoring worship. He is determined to destroy that love, because he will not permit another person—healthy and natural—to sacrifice her life to his blindness. He has come to Naples to fulfill a death pact with his fellow blind officer. Long ago they had agreed, when life became intolerable, to kill themselves.

But at the moment of suicide, our arrogant colonel's courage fails him. He cannot fire the fatal shot. His furious pretense collapses.

He stands exposed as a coward, a blind man who desperately needs—as do all blind people—someone to be his eyes, and his guide, and his strength. And, of course, the girl is waiting. Since girlhood she has sensed their destiny.

A beautiful story, and a shining example of character

drama. The protagonist did what he did because of what he was—a blind hero fighting deathly fear with arrogance. Every move of the plot was his *character in action.*

We could multiply the examples for the rest of the chapter. Among other classics are: *Citizen Kane, Casablanca, Funny Girl, The African Queen, Marty, A Man for All Seasons, All About Eve, A Streetcar Named Desire,* and on and on and on.

What it finally comes down to is this: in most fine plays and films and worthwhile TV stories, the character is the cause and the plot is the effect.

In fact, you will often find, once you have established your protagonist and his adversary, that you're not in charge anymore. *They* are, if they are interesting, compelling individuals. A dominant character may even take over your story, and it will end quite differently than you thought it would.

Characters can develop alarmingly—like kids. We think, because they're ours, that we can lay it all out for them. But when they mature and rebel and begin to do their own thing— then they really begin to live.

The same William Archer, quoted earlier, put it this way, only this time he spoke with wise authority: "The difference between a live play and a dead one is that the plot of the dead play controls the characters, while in the living play, the characters control the plot."

The "dead" play, by this distinction, is the mechanical gimmick drama so typical of the worst of television. As audiences for those sterile episodes we do not identify with human characters: we are simply flung about by the twists of a roller-coaster plot.

There have been endless mechanistic plots since television emerged in the Forties. All are now mercifully forgotten. But in the spanning years we have seen such enduring *character* stories as *The Autobiography of Miss Jane Pittman, Missiles of October, Brian's Song, A Christmas Story, Little Moon of Alban, A Case of Rape,* and *My Sweet Charlie.* The technique is to underlight your plot and spotlight your people.

The characters in great stage and screenplays are the

lifeblood of the craft. They are the memories we carry home from the theater. They are the old friends we return to when we watch revivals. Human characters are where it's been, where it's at, and where it will always be. So that's your work order, if you plan to write film. Play gods and lovers. Make people.

All right. *How?*

Larger Than Life

It has been said that *drama favors the great saint or the great sinner. It seldom deals in the ordinary sizes.*

This aspect began ages ago when the theater of the Greeks originated formal drama. They featured in their casts emperors and their patrician ladies, generals and ethnic heroes, indeed the gods themselves. In Shakespeare's plays the bloodlines of the heroes were often blue—Hamlet, the Kings Henry, Macbeth, Lear, and the rest. Now our twentieth century has seen real-life kings and princesses fall away before the upsurge of the common man. But this new and saltier breed of leading players still has striking and special qualities.

In story conferences for many a TV series you will hear the producer say: "We want larger-than-life characters." He means spies like James Bond, policewomen like Angie Dickinson, pop-offs like Archie Bunker, doctors like Marcus Welby, heroines like Jane Pittman. But such men and women are above the common run; they are not ordinary sizes. They are exceptional figures, and they appeal to their mass audiences as did the kings and queens and gods of long ago.

Drama favors the great saint or the great sinner boils down to this: pick outstanding, appealing, or compelling individuals for your protagonists—such as Lawrence of Arabia, the Godfather, Bonnie and Clyde, Mary Poppins, a Man for All Seasons, Rocky. Do not feature drab, run-of-the-mill personalities; people who are essentially blank and uninteresting. In life you know what you do about nonpeople who bore you. You shun them—and so do audiences.

Now this does *not* mean that you can't write about punks and scrubs and nobodies. Eugene O'Neill, Arthur Miller, all the leading American playwrights and film writers select heroes and heroines from the docks and side streets. But note what they do with them. The characterization of stage figures has been called an exercise in subtle exaggeration.

When a common man dominates a film or play, he often walks taller than a common man. Or he becomes a prototype, the representative of a million common men—like Willie Loman in *Death of a Salesman*, or Stanley Kowalski in *A Streetcar Named Desire*.

This, essentially, is the technique: if your character is a bore, make him a special and interesting bore (such as Peter Falk in "Columbo"). If he's a slob, make him a super-slob. If your woman is a nuisance, make her a fascinating nuisance (Barbra Streisand as the twenty-dollar hooker in *The Owl and the Pussycat*). If your protagonist is a nobody, make him a representative of a million nobodies, and thus he will gain the stature of a universal and tragic somebody. For a shining example, remember Al Pacino in *Dog Day Afternoon*.

The Dominant Characteristic

Give your protagonist a *dominant characteristic*. This may be a selfless dedication, a compulsion, or a terror. It may be her strength, or his tragic flaw. This dominant trait is sometimes called the *character key*, or the *character spine*.

When you go to the producers' offices, they often brief you on what they want for their films or TV episodes. They will tell you with glazed earnestness, "We want characters in depth. We want to know *all* about a character."

That is nonsense. Nobody knows all about Hamlet, or Camille, or the two boys in *Easy Rider*. There is never time for that in any script or film. But what you should know is his or her most significant character trait: be it integrity, courage, compassion—or your choice of the seven deadly sins.

Examples: *Othello*. His jealousy destroyed him. We know

other things about him—and we must—or a character becomes a single-dimension silhouette. Othello was brave, compassionate, and a leader of men. But his dominant characteristic, as far as the play personified him, was jealousy.

The Taming of the Shrew. The title specifies Katharine's dominant characteristic. She was a driving dame—a shrew.

Serpico. An outstanding police picture of the 1973 season. It visualized the true story of a New York cop who wouldn't take a bribe. Serpico staged a one-man war against police corruption, and very nearly got killed for it. His character key was his compulsive honesty—and that powered the whole dramatic story and the TV series that grew out of it.

In the Heat of the Night. Bigotry was the theme—exemplified by the redneck sheriff, played by Rod Steiger. Sidney Poitier also starred. But Steiger was the bigot. His racism was almost all we knew about him, except that the developing plot forced him to face that quality in himself—no small feat for a redneck southern sheriff. And in the end he *did* something about it. He admitted that the black man was the better cop, and he carried Poitier's bag to the railroad station. And he won the Academy Award.

Examples are without number. No analysis can take the time to one-by-one them for you. But the principle endures. And it's not confined to *writing* characterization. An actor in the class, some seasons back, when we reached this point, shot up his hand, excited. He said: "That's it! That's what a director told me. The only director who really explained to me how to develop my performance of a character. He gave me a *central concept* of the man, a dominant trait on which to base my interpretation. And it *worked!* The character became real to me, and I could play him."

Writing a character is much the same thing, only you, the playwright, create the central concept.

So this is one of the higher percentage shots. Start by giving your hero or heroine a compelling characteristic. Then develop and enrich his or her personality around that character key

Out of this dominant trait, this character key, grows the most familiar—and the most important—of all plot lines. Which is:

Character-Change, or Tragic-Flaw, Story

The character-change story is a story written around a hero or heroine with a character hang-up, often called a tragic flaw. The individual is forced to face this tragic fault or weakness and usually, at the story climax, to overcome it.

The coward story is the classic example. But the hero's flaw need not be physical cowardice. It can be any human fear or fault, an insecurity devil, a false judgment, a self-delusion. This flaw is exposed in the early action. As time passes, our protagonist senses it within himself. At the climax he faces up to it and (usually) redeems himself by word and deed. Variations on this theme are infinite, and here are some famous examples.

Guess Who's Coming to Dinner? Spencer Tracy's flaw is confused liberalism. He discovers the truth of tolerance.

My Fair Lady. Professor Higgins, an intellectual snob, becomes a human being.

Midnight Cowboy. Jon Voight decides "there must be an easier way to make a buck."

Marty and *The Apartment.* Ernest Borgnine and Jack Lemmon, in widely different contexts, encounter true love and finally face up to it.

Ruggles of Red Gap. An early film classic in which Charles Laughton, an English valet, lands in the American West and becomes his own man.

The King and I. A Siamese despot (Yul Brynner) discovers a British peculiarity called compassion.

The Hospital. George C. Scott, a great doctor on the brink of suicide, regains his belief in himself.

Why is this character-change plot so oft-repeated in the story spectrum? Perhaps it's due to a primitive response in all of us to the evolution process. There is no convincing proof that we are better than the elephants, but we like to think we are.

Man—the most highly evolved being—has created God, who is unattainable. But mankind has also produced Christ, Muhammad, Buddha, the Virgin Mary—mortals who attained divinity. All the great religions worship humans who became gods. Thus, when we see a striking character on stage or screen gain wisdom, conquer weakness, and emerge a stronger, clearer mortal—we respond emotionally. We have related to that individual and shared his moment of divinity.

Whatever the reason, this character-change or self-discovery story has been the champ since theater began. More great plays for stage, screen, and TV have been written around the formula than any other.

But before we leave it, let's add a word of caution. There is an easy misstep. I have had examples from many classes, and seen it strangely often on the professional screen.

The misstep lies in making your character a total misfit from the beginning. Perhaps a man with scorching antisocial tendencies and no redeeming grace. Or a husband who belittles and beats up his wife and kicks the neighbor's dog. If he rasps their nerves all through the first two acts, the audience will get impatient and decide, "The hell with him." When his character finally does change, they won't believe it because it will seem like a playwright's convenience. Worse than that, they won't give a damn. You've lost them.

There is a simple safeguard. Give him character substance. Your audience must like or admire him enough to *want* him to face that flaw and change. Just don't make him irredeemable. Mix in some positive, appealing qualities along with his tragic flaw. Then the audience will ride with you and pull for that change.

Character Shading

Fine writers present their characters in perspective, like great portrait painters. Living people are not silhouettes, all good or all bad. As you are not, and I am not. Human nature has always been a tortured mix.

Today's audiences are aware of this: they are all unlicensed psychologists anyway. To them an all good guy or good girl as a leading character is old-fashioned. Worse than that, unreal. So is a villain who is all bad, but we will get to villains in a moment. The point is: audiences don't identify with character flatness, because one-dimensional people don't exist in life.

There is a wide range of qualities, good and less than that, in theatrical heroes and heroines. Consider Rhett Butler, Cleopatra, Kojak, Alice, the Midnight Cowboy, and Archie Bunker.

Often a hero's imperfections make him human. For example, President Lincoln, with his strivings against self-doubt, his loathing of war, his struggle to meet the challenge he faced as his country's leader. Or Hamlet's indecision. Or Cyrano de Bergerac. He was a ridiculous paragon of courage, poetry, wit, and constancy. So his playwright-creator Rostand gave him that enormous nose.

The "I Am" Technique

Take a hard look at some big movies and much of television. A lot of those gorgeous or grubby people are skin-deep anybodies. They offer little or nothing but the actor's personality. But in the finer films and TV shows the exciting opposite happens. All the cast people seem varied, human, alive, and special.

The difference lies in the writer's relationship with his brain children. Do you really know this motley family you are rearing? Do you think their jokes are funny? Do you know their inner fears, their dreams, and their fighting weight? Because if you don't, the audience never will. And there is a practical way to find out, which I devised for our UCLA class. We call it the *I am* technique.

Let's say your character's name is Damon Quaid. Type his name at the top of a sheet of paper. Then for a few minutes, you become that character. You describe yourself:

I, Damon Quaid, *am* a white male, twenty-nine, employed by the *Chicago Tribune*.

I am ... (List physical features, height, weight, hair color, eyes, build, etc. Include defects to give the living picture dimension.)

I am ... (List race, nationality, religion.)

I am ... (List social status and life style, income, education, social background, marital status, hobbies, prizes won, police convictions.)

I am ... (List psychological drives and attitudes, moral standards, sex life, character flaws.)

I am ... (List unique or salient traits that make you special and different from those around you. Include a *dominant characteristic*.)

Don't fudge on this. Expand the list. Overdo it. Many of the specifics will not appear in your dramatic story. But such full itemization gives you true personal empathy with Damon Quaid. Knowing him as yourself grants you a kind of *droit du seigneur*. You can dramatize his wedding night, because that was you there in bed with the bride.

A capsule example: you have a story idea about a rich oil magnate who has a delinquent daughter. Make an *I am* list of the girl's good points and her problems. Then impersonate her powerful father, listing his concepts of the marketplace, of life and love. What inside you (that father) might have triggered her decadence? And what qualities, even deeper inside you both, can help her confront her problems in the third act? Those special character traits can be the cornerstone of your whole plot structure.

Your *I am* list should contain more than major attributes. Digging around, you'll often find kinks that you didn't suspect were there. Odd traits and quirks can lend vivid assistance. Such as Jack Benny's stinginess, which he parlayed into a career. Remember Sherlock Holmes, who sniffed cocaine and kept saying "Elementary, my dear Watson."

Likewise, Archie Bunker's mangling of the English language. His fractured grammar also reminds us there is little that is startlingly new in stage and film character writing. A great English playwright did just the same thing a couple of hundred years ago in a classic called *The Rivals*.

The character was Mrs. Malaprop in Richard Brinsley Sheridan's high comedy. She mangled the English language in the same manner that Archie Bunker does. She's remembered fondly even in the dictionary, where a *malapropism* is defined as a "ridiculous confusion of language." And she got the same big laughs that Archie gets.

Woody Allen is haunted through most of his pictures by girl trouble. So was Marty. Rhoda's love-hungry sister can't stop stuffing herself with food. A famous western killer was riddled with superstitions, and they finally destroyed him.

Never disdain these classic strategems. They humanize a character with quirks to which every audience can relate. They are the devices with which Pennsylvania Avenue popularizes presidents. Our present leader pitches softball, and everybody calls him Jimmy. The aristocratic, intellectual President Roosevelt liked to relax with his martini before dinner. General Eisenhower was a fly fisherman. Years ago President Coolidge, a cold personality hard to popularize, also went fishing. But to attract the mass vote, he fished with worms!

Remember that drama favors the great saint or the great sinner—heroes and rascals who are above the common run. But they must still be as welcome in the village pub as in the manor house. To put mass audiences at ease writers often give their people what a popular western producer called "Howdy traits." He meant down-to-earth characteristics, small compulsions, human eccentricities, recognition qualities. These set up what is known as *empathy*.

Empathy occurs when your thoughts and emotions identify with those of another person. Call it emotional interlock, self-sharing. Sensitive characterization develops a bond between the people on the screen and the audience in the seats.

For an hour or two those screen people and their problems become partly you and yours. Say a writer creates a drama for six characters. Sixty million people flock to the theaters not just to watch them perform, but to slip into their souls and skins, and to live those six parts. That is dramatic empathy.

Character Clichés

Character clichés strew the dreariest stretches of TV wasteland. The new cop, or the new private eye, or the new doctor seem to be nothing but composites of all the others. All the others, remember, have long since worn out their welcome and been canceled.

Oddly enough, the television bosses, not the writers, are basically responsible. Network tycoons are not promoting creative art; they are selling commercial time. Their series stars and stories are rooted in clichés because the masses feel comfortable with them. Such public acceptance generates gigantic profits. No realist in a profit-motive economy can expect judicious executives to bet on long shots like originality and inspiration. That would be irresponsible.

Accordingly, every TV series and virtually every script filters through network controls. Writers fly courses that they are advised to fly, and they land where the tower tells them to land. A leading result is that most of the best serious dramatists flee television the first chance they get to write feature films.

On the big movie screens different standards prevail. Box-office appeal is the yardstick; originality can be worth millions. Contrary to the carbon-copy taint of TV, the distinction of great screen roles lies in their creativity. Think of the Hunchback of Notre Dame, Citizen Kane, Bonnie and Clyde, Mr. Chips, Funny Girl, King Kong, Doctor Zhivago, Rhett Butler and Scarlett O'Hara, Marty, Shane, and the Godfather. Think of them, and then blank them out of your mind completely. Because the key to character originality is to reject memories.

The tragedy of hack writers is that they cop out on their own creative gifts. When they settle for rewriting another playwright's people—say the names are Romeo or Rosalind—they come out with pale clichés. Because no one can ever write them as Shakespeare did.

But if you have the guts to be totally honest, nobody can write a character exactly as you can. The only true original personality that you can put into a script is you.

Secondary Characters

There is another grubby area where cliché characters gather. It is not confined to television, but is the blight of many a feature movie. It lies in the lower end of the cast list, where the second- and third-string actors work. The dreariest character clichés in all films and TV appear in those minor parts. They are the likes of the slangy waitress, the faceless desk clerk, the squealing teenager, the stupid, sadistic sheriff. Writers appear to be caricaturing other writers' clichés. Uncritical producers and directors seem not to sense the difference.

For the most obvious example of the obvious, take the descriptive "a sexy blonde." A fifty-year-old cliché, this has come to mean almost nothing. In its place, describe your character as a distinct personality, special, different from the other girls. She just happens, as well, to be sexy and blonde.

In a similar sense, do not expect an audience to identify with "an average secretary." But they will line up with Miss X, a complex, appealing—or obnoxious—girl who happens to work as a secretary.

Never allow these cliché small-part people to dilapidate your screenplay. Again, the key is to respect each character in your script as you respect yourself. Present them all as different, vibrant, special human beings. Incidentally, actors will love you for it.

Study films and plays by the great writers. An unmistakable mark of a master craftsman is that he individualizes *all* his characters. For a brilliant example, however, I am picking a TV situation comedy. Since television is the stockroom of clichés, I am especially glad to cite this exception which for years proved the rule.

Our example is "The Mary Tyler Moore Show." Now departed, it will outlive many of us in reruns. Remember how every single person on the screen through all those years conveyed a special, individual quality. Several of them were so distinctive that they became stars in series of their own. This meant brilliant writing (and producing, directing, and acting). Mary herself was a radiant star. But as a co-producer, she had the guts and insight to realize that great surrounding characters would make her own part shine that much brighter.

The Antagonist, the Heavy, the Bad Guy

Never neglect or underestimate the importance of your villain. "It is the character of the antagonist," it has been shrewdly noted, "that drives your story toward catastrophe."

Beyond that, brilliant characterization of the bad guy can add inches to the stature of your hero. For the best illustration, let's do our research in reverse. Say you pick, as your villain, a gutless pigeon, a gabby, twitching nobody. Your protagonist needs little heroic savvy to wipe him out. He almost has to stoop to do it. But if the heavy is a corrupt genius, towering with boodle and clout, then your hero must chop a lot of wood to bring him down. Witness Woodward and Bernstein, two obscure newsmen who became national heroes. They did a brilliant job on Watergate, granted. But the angle that finally secured their place in history was the caliber of their antagonist.

There is an even more essential aspect to villain design than just giving him muscle. Power and savagery have become standard equipment for big-screen bad guys. In fact, many heavies become clichés because they are painted all flat black. The cure is to mix in kinks of human kindness.

Think of *The Godfather Part II*. The Godfather was, of

course, bad guy and protagonist—the story's central figure. See what they did with him to make him a mortal to whom audiences could relate. They used one of the oldest tricks in the melodrama writer's book. The Godfather was madly in love with his wife and kids. That was his ultimate tragedy, because he lost them. He was a revolting murderer. But he was *human*.

Another example, quoted by author-teacher Lajos Egri, from some forgotten drama. The antagonist of the story was a ruthless woman, a bloody bitch—but with a weak spot. She was terrified of growing old. She compensated by being always warm and thoughtful with old people. She had feelings. She was human.

Perhaps the most eminent of all villains is Shylock in *The Merchant of Venice.* He was a moneylender who proposed to exact a pound of living flesh for an unpaid bill. This is a *monster!* In the underworld they still call loan sharks "Shylocks."

But remember what Shakespeare did to make him human. He revealed the injustice of man that had made Shylock vindictive. "Hath not a Jew eyes? If you prick us, do we not bleed? If you poison us, do we not die? And if you wrong us, shall we not revenge?"

Bitterly as audiences hate Shylock, at the same time they can't help feeling sympathy for him. And that is why he is one of the immortals of dramatic literature.

This, then, is the simple recipe for the care and feeding of your antagonist.

Along with a full set of burglar's tools, give him mortal *emotions* and *feelings.*

Although your heavy is a horror, make him or her also a vulnerable human being.

Just don't make him too bad to be true!

Deeper Aspects

Characterization unlocks the hiding places of the heart and mind. Most of us spend a lot of our lives covering up. Babies grab for anything they want, and go to the bathroom wherever they happen to be. But in our early years discipline, which is necessary for us to live in an ordered society, sets in. Adult life is a constant compromise between what we crave and what we can achieve. We are all wearing gamblers' masks most of the time.

A basic fascination in watching plays, movies, and TV is seeing people discard these masks. A play is the revelation of a character caught in a crisis. He or she reacts primitively, truthfully. The pressures inside are such that the safety valve has got to blow.

This requires that you, the author, go deep, and report from the secret places. You reveal the intimate moments, which in life are played privately—the moments of fear that we always hide, the foolish little things, the mistakes that people would laugh at. Also the fateful moments of decision and sacrifice. Good characterization is the art of decent and indecent exposure.

The playwright is like a priest who has listened to men and women kneeling in his confession box. Then he offers their secrets as a warning, or an inspiration, a challenge, perhaps a beacon of hope, to those who watch his plays.

Summation

There is only one of you in the world. And only one of me. All men and women on this earth were born different, inimitable human beings. Look around the supermarket, the classroom, or the family dinner table.

But we are all, also, typical people—in our essentials the same and universal. We all get hungry, and love, and hate, and dream, and fight when cornered. We are all Everyman and Everywoman.

So this is the ultimate prescription:

A character in a play should combine the qualities of (1) a unique individual *and* (2) a universal human being.

Write a man or woman or a child who is everybody, but who becomes in your dramatic story an absorbing variation, a striking original.

Do this truthfully, and you will sell your script. Because it has been wisely written that *the greatest plot in the world is a human being*.

3.

CONFLICT

The Working Substance of Drama and Comedy

If you stop passersby on Hollywood Boulevard and ask them to define *drama*, you'll get a lot of dingbat answers. Despite the fact that most of the passersby on Hollywood Boulevard are screenwriters. Or, perhaps, because of it.

Just what is drama?

The most practical definition that I know was given by the French critic Fernand Brunetière. Having studied the theater for a good part of his life, he narrowed it down to this:

"Drama is the representation of the will of man in conflict."

This may sound obvious, dry, and scholastic. Don't worry. It is. It comes from the gaslit long ago when critics of the legitimate theater were a rare and august breed. In those days, movie theaters, television and radio networks didn't even exist. Credentialed critics regarded the theater not as a carnival that never closes, but as a Master Art. Brunetière, writing for his perceptive readers in Paris, said this, in greater detail, about conflict:

The theater in general is nothing but a place for the development of the human will, attacking the obstacles opposed to it by Destiny, Fortune or circumstance. .. Drama [and this obviously now includes film and TV drama] ... is the representation of the will of man in conflict. It is *one of us* thrown living upon the stage, there to struggle against his fellow mortals, against himself, if need be; against history and social law, against the ambitious, the self interests; against the prejudice, the folly, the malevolence of those who surround him.

This is a diagnosis made almost a hundred years ago. Does it apply to the modern patient? Does it still work for a $5 million movie, or for a fast hour of felony television?

In writing a motion picture or a TV script, your object is not just to amuse yourself or to provide strangers with reading matter for a quiet evening. Your purpose is to devise a dream experience that will induce millions of people to devote to your work from one to three hours of their allotted time on earth. You've got to tear them away from books, conversation, music, the Super Bowl, sex, and the dinner dishes. What major chord in human nature do you play on to do this?

You play on people's instinctive absorption in watching other people fight it out. This suggests that conflict is telepathic, a shared happening.

Each one of us, in earlier incarnations, has fought for food, for habitation, for threatened loved ones. Dim echoes of these primal struggles haunt us, drawing us to conflict as a ritual of the survival pattern.

Consider the simplest, daily example. A couple of street kids square off and start slugging each other. People on both sidewalks pause to look. All ages crane their necks; heedless males crowd around, cheering the kids on. Old ladies cluck disapproval. But all—by some conditioned reflex—have stopped for that moment and become spectators. And *that is reason one* why you write your film. So millions of people on life's sidewalks will stop and crane their necks. So they will become spectators.

Producers and promoters, who live off spectators, know all about this reflex. The highest purses of all public exhibitions are earned by boxers and bullfighters. People pay millions of dollars to watch, in comforting safety, a bloody conflict in which a fellow human can get his brains knocked out, or, in the bullring, be killed.

On the full conflict canvas, war stories are the most obvious, most primitive. But war is only a formalization of individual survival struggle. Man's conflict against death is the dramatic key to just about all the exploration and discovery, sea, air, and space, crime, conquest, rescue, pioneering, and action-adventure dramas ever staged or filmed.

But swiftly and emphatically let us take notice that conflict need not involve broken heads and shattered corpses. In short, violence.

A hushed courtroom can be the arena of bitter conflict. In fact, the judicial process was created to resolve conflicts *without* violence. Yet how often have you seen a murder trial hold a theater audience spellbound?

Perhaps our oldest standby for bloodless conflict is the hearthside. The battle of the sexes has been fought on stage and screen and tube ten thousand times and will be fought forever. Primitive conflict fires up in any three-cornered love story. A gathering of the bereaved after a burial may end up in a battle royal. Family feuds are undying.

Our example in this domestic arena is a classic of American stage and screen. Without bloodshed or gunfire, it was packed with two hours of the most savage male-female conflict in theatrical literature. Its title: *Who's Afraid of Virginia Woolf?*

The simplest conflict design, in generic terms, is to present two major characters with wills opposed. One, classically, represents good will, and the other ill will. Your drama recounts the struggle between them and climaxes when one defeats the other.

Does this seem simplistic? Why are we wasting time on such bromides?

Because we have just sketched the conflict design of *Hamlet*, the greatest play in English, and *Gone with the Wind*, probably the greatest motion picture.

There are, literally, unnumbered others. Surely the majority of worthwhile and popular films ever produced illustrate Brunetière's concept. It is not just a dusty axiom. "The will of man in conflict" boils down to a master essence of playwriting.

This concept goes far beyond personal conflict plots. High on the list is the story in which the hero's purpose clashes with prejudice or convention, or social law. These were Galileo's conflicts, Christ's, Louis Pasteur's, Martin Luther King's, and Joan of Arc's. In any social comedy where the heroine from the wrong side of the tracks yearns to marry the senator's son, she confronts social prejudice. Which hardy pattern has proven itself all the way from *Cinderella* to *Funny Girl* to *The Sound of Music* to *Guess Who's Coming to Dinner?*

There is a useful technique for crafting this type of material. Convention and social law are faceless villains. But a live antagonist can stand tough on the screen and play conflict scenes with your hero.

Therefore, personalize prejudice. Cast your villain as a leader of ignorance or bigotry. Make him a Goliath of intolerance. Paint him as so powerful that your David seems to have no chance. Then your audience will be pulling hard for small David, since he has guts and truth on his side. He keeps fighting, and finally he wipes out Goliath. That is exactly what Sidney Poitier did in *In the Heat of the Night*. The audience loved it, and the film won the Academy Award.

The deluge of disaster pictures in the Seventies has highlighted another conflict subspecies. That is man against nature or cataclysm. Examples that have drawn millions of spectators and shaken thousands of theater walls are *Earthquake*, *The Poseidon Adventure*, *The Towering Inferno*, and *Jaws*.

Such situations can be harder to dramatize than they look on the billboards. You can't write an entire film about crashing masonry or an erupting volcano. Nature, like social prejudice, is impersonal. She can starve you, squash you, or drown you, but she can't verbalize it. An entire picture against a disembodied, voiceless antagonist becomes repetitive.

The remedy is quick and obvious. Weave a human story through the cataclysm sequences.

Every one of the man-against-nature epics has an elaborate "people plot." Remember *Jaws* and *Jaws 2* with all that formidably forgettable material about the summer resort and its people? Remember *Robinson Crusoe?* Why do you think Defoe introduced Friday? He did it to give Crusoe someone besides the sand and voiceless sea with whom to play scenes.

Clint Eastwood did a minor film in 1975 called *The Eiger Sanction.* Eastwood and others were climbing a jagged Swiss mountain peak. The conflict was visually ideal, since man seems so tiny and futile against the cruel immensity of the mountain. Climbing scenes were breathtaking. But they would also have become monotonous if the mountain was your hero's sole antagonist. Fortunately, the plot revealed that some of his fellow climbers had lured Eastwood up there to do him in. This doubled his danger—the overwhelming threat of nature, plus human barbarity. In the third act, of course, Eastwood blew the bad guys off the mountain. But the double jeopardy kept the plot alive. The conflict played.

For a final example we have *Deliverance*, a scary film mentioned in another context earlier. A group of city guys set out on a vacation trip down a dangerous wilderness river. The river, by itself, is rampant enough to demolish or drown them all. But halfway down the playwright adds human heavies to the natural antagonist. A couple of spooky, mountain-grown homosexuals capture and rape one of the city party, and our friends have to kill to survive. But the dead are cronies of the local hillbilly sheriff. Now our heroes are in doubly dangerous waters; as well as a rampaging river, they face a murder rap. Thus human malevolence compounds a purely natural conflict.

When the river danger began to get boring, human conflict kicked the dramatic story interest back into gear.

Still a fourth and constantly useful conflict pattern develops when your hero's enemy is himself. These are the antagonist-within stories. "I have met the enemy, and he is me."

Dr. Jekyll and Mr. Hyde is our constant example. A wise, humane man combined with an evil beast in the same person. *Hamlet* is also of this school: his own indecision is almost as dangerous to his purpose as is the malignant king. *Five Easy Pieces*, a film that won an Academy Award nomination for Jack Nicholson, was a brilliant study of such inner conflict.

The character-change, or tragic-flaw, story fits into this conflict category. Plaguing the protagonist are fear, greed, or whichever of the deadly sins seems to be driving him to disaster. But opposing his tragic flaw are positive forces. He mobilizes these forces and fights to redeem his self-respect.

A distinguishing factor of this tragic-flaw story is, usually, that no tangible villain appears in the cast of characters. Good guy and bad guy combine in the same person. Dr. Jekyll solved his inner conflict by suicide, thus destroying Mr. Hyde, who was, of course, his evil ego. In *The Hospital*, Paddy Chayefsky's Academy Award–winning screenplay, George C. Scott played a distinguished New York doctor who had lost faith in himself. But he met a girl, as did Chayefsky's seriocomic hero Marty. Both found a new self-belief in love.

Since with *Marty* we are edging into comedy, let's salute the obvious. As far back as the Greeks, the *commedia dell'arte*, and Punch and Judy, virtually all comedies have been based on conflict. This is so evident that it needs no deliberation. Simply a few classic examples:

The Taming of the Shrew. Even the title expresses the story conflict.

Peter Pan. Many lesser conflicts are climaxed in the battle between Peter and the fearful pirate, Captain Hook.

M*A*S*H. Pervasive conflict between the old army and the new.

"I Love Lucy." Classic husband-wife conflict. Although

one of the earliest situation comedies, it is still playing on television in the wee small daytime hours.

Conflict has been called the working substance of drama. *Working substance* is a term in mechanics denoting the fluid (gas or steam) that—under pressure—makes the machine move. Conflict generates pressures which make your dramatic vehicle move!

Here are some of the special techniques that writers use to create it.

Introduce Your Opposition Early

Conflict is hearsay until the antagonist appears. The bullfight is an elemental example. The opening formalities of music and pageantry is attractive packaging. But when the heavy wooden doors open and the raging black animal charges into the ring to kill the matador—then the roars rise. The ancient ritual of life or death has begun.

This audience response is so swift and instinctive that a majority of crime melodramas open with the evil genius or the evil deed. The beginning of "Columbo," for example, devotes itself to in-depth characterization of the killer, and photographic detail of the murder. Only then, and not until then, does Columbo shuffle in to restore order.

This general pattern, long a standard in detective fiction, spreads far beyond paperback books and popular television. Many a modern big-screen movie starts with a shock teaser *even before the opening titles. All the President's Men* began with the Watergate burglary. *The Godfather Part II* started with mayhem in Sicily.

Admittedly, it is often not possible to open your story with a shock teaser. Or, indeed, with the shark, or the murderer's entrance. But when his arrival is too long delayed, your first act tends to become impassive, static.

Let's accent the point with a reverse example of national folk drama. As much as many women and sophisticates detest football, the Super Bowl draws among the biggest television

audiences of the modern year. Why? Because it is an orches-
trated spectacle of raw mental and physical conflict.

Yet the author-producer network dares to insult that potential audience with a first act of stupefying boredom. In
January 1977 they introduced owners, coaches, officials, players, and fans in saloons for over *seventy minutes*. Then, it
seemed, they did it all over again from the blimp.

Such a blare of trumpets quickly turns into less flattering
sounds. Bored, impatient spectators tune to other networks or
go out to drink beer or wash the dog. But, in droves, they come
back to their TV sets just before kickoff. Because that's when
the head-knocking starts. The conflict!

The lesson for scriptwriters—including those who never
watch football—is explicit. Streamline your introductions.
Move into your dramatic conflict as early as possible—with the
kickoff.

Don't introduce it, and explain it. *Do it!*

Conflict in Individual Scenes

Among the first things playwrights learn to toss overboard are
social grace and training. From childhood we are all taught
"Don't spit in the other kid's eye." But dramatic protagonists
must! Usually the bad kid takes the first shot. But from then on
your hero must fight back, or both he and your precious drama
will be wiped out. His fighting back is the overall plot struggle:
the start-to-finish conflict structure that every play must have.

But there is a second type of conflict that offers unfailing
values. That is subconflict, which you inject into *individual*
scenes.

For example: your heroine is having tea and gossip at
home with the girls. They are discussing the handsome new
doctor in town, and how half the single women are blissed out.
Someone has called this *sewing-circle dialogue*, and it can flat-
ten your dramatic interest like a leak in a tire.

Plug that leak with subconflict. Perhaps one of the heroine's friends had a spin with this medic back at USC. She can't

bear him! The girls get into a flap. You characterize the doctor, fly storm warnings, and the audience stops crunching popcorn. Because conflict plays!

Or perhaps you've placed a group of terrorists outside a rural airport waiting to hijack an incoming plane. But the plane is delayed and the bad guys are drinking and killing time. They are also killing your dramatic interest. Inject subconflict. One paranoid killer takes one drink too many, and questions the boss terrorist's strategy. An ugly confrontation flares. Audience attention peaks as the doomed plane is heard circling overhead to land.

Such character subconflicts have been standbys of classic TV series. Remember the irascible Dr. Casey, who could juice up any medical discussion by contradicting his chief of staff? In most police television series the hero has a hardmouthed superior who turns police procedure scenes into dog-eat-dog disputes. A "Gunsmoke" staple for fifteen years was Sheriff Matt Dillon's insult crossfire with Doc or Festus.

All comedy series depend on it. How about Ted Baxter and Lou Grant in "The Mary Tyler Moore Show"? Or Rhoda vs. Rhoda's mother? Or Archie vs. Meathead?

Study the films and TV shows that you see in coming evenings. Consult your interest meter. Time and again you will find that when your attention wilts, it is in scenes where the conflict weakens.

Rate your own work accordingly. Search it out, scene by scene, for interest lags, low spots. Make them high spots. Nothing will cure all the ills of scriptwriting, but until a better snake oil comes along, turn to conflict. Everybody else in the writing trade does, including Sophocles, George Bernard Shaw, and Shakespeare.

Confrontation Scenes

Confrontation scene is a familiar term in TV story conferences. At Warner Brothers TV it used to be defined as "two guys sticking out their jaws at each other." Two gentle ladies can be just as deadly, or two shrieking tarts.

Uproar is not essential. More great confrontation scenes play in courtrooms than in western saloons. A confrontation scene is usually a two-character head-on clash. Neither holds anything back. Face to face. Hully gully. *Confrontation scenes play!*

Exposition Scenes

Exposition scenes are also called the *back story*. Briefly, they describe the background of the play's characters and their status in the dramatic situation. Such exposition scenes are defined and discussed in Chapter 6, "Beginning Your Screenplay."

This back story often gets gluey with detail and stagnates your first act. Yet you must set up your characters and their emotional interlocks. You must inform the audience about happenings before the story started. But audiences don't want to be informed. They have paid money to see *what happens next.* Thus, exposition scenes rank among the worst enemies of young inexperienced playwrights. Also of middle-aged professional playwrights. Plodding pages of exposition can stop any author's drama dead.

Again, the remedy is at hand. Reach for that vial on your desk—conflict.

For example: a man and his wife witness a neighborhood murder. He is stuffed with self-importance; her head is stuffed with feathers. Cops arrive to question them. Their answers are essential to brief your audience on the background of the dead man and neighborhood motives for his killing. But as man and wife give those answers, they contradict each other. They get mad and squall it out. Their human discord delights the audience. Absorbed by the conflict, viewers happily accept the dull back story exposition.

The example is primary. The precept is comprehensive.

When you *must* brief your audience on an interstate bus schedule, don't put a glum actor on camera to read the time table slowly aloud to them. Bring in a couple of characters who dislike each other. One has astigmatism, and drops his glasses. In the uproar, they spell out the needed information.

Conflict in Love Scenes

Love scenes can be deceptively difficult to write. "I love you" is the oldest chestnut on the writer's shelf. Ten minutes of blissful agreement on the giant screen can get pretty dreary.

Once again, summon conflict. It's an ancient device, but this is its special aspect: it is so deeply ingrained that it seems timeless.

Remember that great first act of *Funny Girl*, where Streisand and Sharif were meeting and falling in love? Remember those abrasive courting scenes between Ali MacGraw and Ryan O'Neal in *Love Story?*

In *My Fair Lady* Rex Harrison and Audrey Hepburn endure three acts of conflict, until they finally face the awful comprehension that they are in love.

What is revered by millions as the greatest film for all screens and all seasons was such a three-hour conflict love scene. A biting, slashing male dog vs. female cat fight from beginning to end. Remember Rhett Butler vs. Scarlett O'Hara in *Gone with the Wind*.

Positive Conflict vs. the Negative or "Prevent" Type

In action-adventure plots, the *positive* type of conflict usually hooks an audience quicker and holds them longer than the *prevent* type. A prevent story plants a bomb under a crowded stadium; the hero cops can't announce it on the loudspeaker because a hundred thousand people would panic. They work through the plot to *prevent* the bomb from blowing up all those spectators.

A more mobile example might be your villain's plot to kidnap the engineer's daughter and escape with her on the train. But the hero lawman *prevents* the kidnapping and impounds the train. This will play as visually less rewarding than the bad guy's snatching train and girl and steaming off across Texas. The hero has to pursue, and save the girl just before the train plunges into a gorge.

See the difference?

This is not to say that the prevent type can be filed in your trash basket. It has worked magic in too many third acts since playwriting began. When a child faces brutal rape, or human life is in the balance (surgery, capital punishment), the prevent type is, clearly, classic.

But modern films and TV specials accent the great outdoors and sweeping visual action. In such contexts, if you plant TNT under a tower or dam, audiences expect you to blow it up. When you promise them the end of this shaky world, give it to them.

Right on Both Sides

Often peak conflict is generated by strong currents of right on both sides.

A mercy killing breeds such a conflict. Can a compassionate doctor, however ethical, refuse death to a patient in terminal agony?

In *Casablanca* Ingrid Bergman and Humphrey Bogart reignite an old love. But Paul Henreid, her husband, depends on her totally in his underground struggle against Nazi tyranny. Shall she opt for human brotherhood, or Humphrey Bogart?

Perhaps your war hero is flying his last mission before going home. He receives orders to firebomb an enemy hospital. Shall he be a traitor to his conscience or his country?

The heights of emotional drama dwell in these scenes that plead truth from opposed points of view. Such conflicts, you will find, play with a special luminous power.

Your Faithful Friend

Conflict has a congenial characteristic for every film or TV writer. It is clear, it is recognizable, it is specific. Your scenes either have it or they don't have it. If they don't, you can often rework them and inject it. Because conflict is not a mystic tool of genius, like mood, or charm, or lyric poetry. Conflict is rude and earthborn. Every film or TV writer can create it by a conscious act of will.

Any man in your script can get tough, or any female bitchy, by a scribble of your pen. And if your scene is lagging, they had better. Because the moment fur starts flying, that scene will start to play.

Conflict is your rowdy, subtle, refined, explosive, and unfailing friend.

Use it!

Retrospect

Never dismiss conflict as some roughhouse technique of movies and television. It goes back through Eugene O'Neill, George Bernard Shaw, Ibsen, and Shakespeare to the birth years of dramatic writing.

I once had a Greek-American student who listened to this discussion and figured that he'd better research it. He was a gifted guy, who has since sold a movie to Columbia. He was also an expert on the ancient Greek classical drama. That, of course, was where modern playwriting started.

So he went home that week and dug through his library of Aeschylus, Sophocles, and Euripides in native Greek. He came back to our next meeting with this report. He told the class that these conflict principles, which power *M*A*S*H*, *Mutiny on the Bounty*, "Roots," and *Star Wars*, were present throughout all the great Greek classic dramas.

Those were written over two thousand years ago. Basic playwriting doesn't change very much.

4.

SUSPENSE

Romeo and Juliet as a Cliff-hanger

The term *suspense story* is generally used to describe a grisly Gothic tale, a spooky murder, or any acute attack of dramatic goose pimples. But such a definition is too confining; in fact it's foggy nonsense. Because most of the dramatic stories that have ever been written are suspense stories.

Romeo and Juliet, for example, is the theater's most cherished love poem. The clinical fact is that it is a suspense drama. How did Shakespeare manage that, under all those hypnotic violins? We will answer that by breaking down the play as a cliff-hanger.

But first let's check out narrative storytelling, as practiced over back fences, from bar stools, or in newspapers. Usually it starts with the headline fact—AXE MURDERER CAPTURED—and then beguiles you at length with facts, figures, quotations, and details. Have you ever noticed how often you do *not* turn to page 11, column 4, to absorb all those details?

The dramatic storyteller employs more seductive techniques. He lures you with a minor (first-act) crisis, and proceeds to a major threat of third-act catastrophe. In the broadest sense, he plants a bomb—physical or emotional—and then saves the explosion for the finish. Thus he generates drama's energy charge, which is suspense.

Jaws is a memorable example. Early in the film the great white shark eats a female bather alive. The writers and director then lead you on a ninety-minute sea-chase until they blow that big white shark to bits. To revel in those ninety minutes, audiences worldwide paid over $200 million. That amounts to some of the loudest box-office applause since storytelling started. It was in response to just one thing—raw suspense.

Suspense begins when security is threatened. Of the ten biggest box-office smashes in screen history,* six used danger of death as their major energy charge. But fear of death has many spidery cousins: foreboding, anxiety, self-doubt, apprehension, shyness, horror. In women's stories fear of death as a suspense device can even be replaced by fear of unwelcome pregnancy.

Suspense sustains soap opera and Walt Disney. Fairy and children's tales bet their piggy banks on it. Shakespeare used it in every play. To illustrate, we are going to dissect *Romeo and Juliet* as a cliff-hanger.

Cliff-hanger, of course, is a term from the earliest movie serials. They bore lurid titles like *The Perils of Pauline* and *The House of Hate*. They were one- or two-reel dramas, each episode ending, metaphorically, with the heroine hanging by her lacquered fingernails to the rim of the thousand-foot cliff. A title would flash on screen inviting the audience to come back next week and see if Pauline perished or was rescued by the heroic Stainless Steele.

Other favorite fade-outs found her lashed to the railroad track in a blizzard, with the Northwest Limited bearing down

* According to *Variety*, as of January 1, 1979, the fabulous ten are: *Star Wars, Jaws, The Godfather, Grease, The Exorcist, The Sound of Music, The Sting, Close Encounters of the Third Kind, Gone with the Wind,* and *Saturday Night Fever.*

through the storm. Or perhaps the setting is the theater and a magician is about to perform his fabulous illusion, "Sawing a Girl in Half." But the audience knows something that he doesn't know. The villain has jammed the machinery, and Pauline is *really* going to be sawed in half.

The purpose of that profitable nonsense was to pique the audience's interest so sharply that viewers would return to the nickelodeon week after week to see what befell poor Pauline. But, oddly, it wasn't nonsense, though it was profitable. Those five-cent tickets now cost up to five dollars. The same cliff-hanger technique is still used in any movie where the director poises his heroine on the brink of rape and then cuts to the cop on the corner busting a jaywalker. Suspense is as old as the theater. *Romeo and Juliet* is a shameless love story, sentimental beyond compare, and this is how William Shakespeare told that love story in primary suspense terms.

Romeo and Juliet
As a Cliff-hanger

In Verona two leading families, the Montagues and the Capulets, are deadly enemies.

Romeo (a Montague) crashes a masked ball given by the Capulets. Himself masked, circulating among the guests, he meets a beautiful girl. Impassioned love at first sight. He asks for a kiss, gets it, and at that point the girl is hurried away by her nurse. Romeo now learns that she is Juliet, cherished daughter of the enemy Capulets.

Suspense hook. If he pursues his love, he's doomed to death. Come back next week and see what happens.

Unable to sleep, the love-sick hero goes to Juliet's balcony that night. Tension: does she love him? Unexpectedly, she appears on the balcony above and declares her love to the moon and stars. Wow. Relief! She not only loves him, she will marry him. How? When? Where? Increasing suspense. So great is their love that they're willing to tempt fate and death.

Come back next week, and see what happens.

Their marriage is arranged through a certain Friar Laurence. Secret daytime ceremony. Minor suspense when we think it isn't coming off. But it does; they're married. Juliet has to hurry back home. But they promise to meet that night. Relief—the course of true love seems to have a chance.

But: later that day Romeo and a comrade called Mercutio are cruising the streets when they meet an enemy Capulet named Tybalt. He insults comrade Mercutio. Romeo tries to cool it because of the marriage, but Mercutio attacks Tybalt. Tybalt kills Mercutio. Bound by honor to avenge his friend, Romeo draws and kills Tybalt. Uproar in Verona! The Prince of Verona banishes Romeo from the city.

Suspense soars. Now what will happen to the lovers? Momentary relief that night. Romeo meets his bride Juliet for a few hours of happiness. Then he heads into exile in the neighboring city of Mantua.

Come back next week and see what happens.

What happens is that Shakespeare doubles the tension. Juliet's father decides it's high time for her to marry. He has even picked out her husband, an eligible, noble type called Paris. Arranged marriages were the custom of Italy; the parents' decision was law. Juliet pleads and protests touchingly. But, of course, she can't confess her real objection. If she did, Romeo would be pursued and killed. Old Dad is obdurate. She must marry Paris.

Rising tension. The distracted Juliet seeks out Friar Laurence. He suggests a miraculous remedy. It's ridiculous, but when the audience is in taut suspense, they'll accept most anything. The Friar gives Juliet a magic potion, which will put her in a trance, seemingly dead. Her body, according to custom, will be laid out in a chapel, and in an open tomb. The Friar will notify Romeo to rescue her by night, and flee with her into romantic exile.

Again relief from tension. Now there is still hope. Come back next week and see what happens.

The worst happens. The Friar's message to Mantua fails to reach Romeo. Meanwhile the devoted Juliet has taken the magic potion. In Verona her death is proclaimed.

Bad news travels fast. Romeo hears the dreadful tidings. He returns, with a vial of poison, to die in the chapel at the tomb of his love.

Note: If the plot seems to be getting mock heroic and overly quaint, remember what George Bernard Shaw said about the magic of Shakespeare: "You can just forget the book, and listen to the music."

The drama approaches catastrophe. Juliet is laid out in the open tomb, apparently dead. Romeo arrives in the candled gloom of the chapel. He sees his bride on the bier in her funeral robes. Notice the added suspense device. He thinks she is dead. We know she isn't!

Now another male figure appears in the chapel shadows. Romeo supposes that he is an enemy Capulet. They fight, and Romeo kills him. Then he discovers that it is Paris, an old friend. Now he is a double murderer, as well as a bereaved lover. Kneeling by Juliet, he takes leave of her with a kiss, and drinks his vial of poison.

In this crisis, Juliet begins to come back through the mists. Friar Laurence arrives, having learned that his letter to Romeo was never received. Juliet, revived, sees her lifeless husband beside her. Sensing what has happened, she tries to kiss the poison from his lips. When this fails, she snatches Romeo's dagger and kills herself.

Their families arrive. Appalled by the tragedy, they agree to cool their feud and live in peace.

Curtain of cliff-hanger. Also finale of one of the tenderest love stories ever written. One which proved its eternal appeal in the film version done by Franco Zeffirelli just a few years ago. The plot was the classic love story suspense pattern. Will the lovers make it, or won't they?

Remember how here and there in this suspense résumé, we used the word *relief*. That, too, is most important. Indeed, it is a must factor. Because high suspense usually follows a design peculiarly its own. It's called *the tension and relief* pattern. The graph goes something like the one at the right.

This graph pattern means that the suspense goes in spurts and stops. It does *not* proceed on a level—no matter how acute the tension at that level. Reason: a spectator's nerves can take only so much. If you key him too high, or stretch him too tight, and then just keep him up there, those nerves may wear out. Your play will make him uncomfortable, and he will begin to dislike it.

Example: a prize fight. The boy in white trunks is your protégé. The tough mug champion knocks him flat. He gets up. Again he's knocked back on his white trunks, *and again.* He's got guts, but that's about all. Bleeding and helpless, he still staggers to his feet. You scream for the referee to stop it, before he gets killed. Because he's your boy; you identify with him. *You're* getting knocked to pieces—steadily, relentlessly—and after a while you just can't take that beating.

That is tension *without* relief. Beyond a point, it stretches you too tight emotionally. You can't endure it.

But: let's say your fighter gets knocked down, but bounces up. Now he flattens the tough mug ... relief ... you cheer. Then *bam!* white trunks goes down again. This time he's hurt. Tension. You gasp. He gets up, clinches, belts the bad guy. Relief ... he still can win. And so it goes. Relief and tension, until the climax, the final round. Your boy is knocked apparently stiff and the referee is counting ten over him. Ultimate tension: point of no return.

Miraculously he beats the count, scrambles up, and knocks the tough champ clear out of the ring! You whoop with relief and delight. The agony of tension is over. You've won and—because of the *relief interludes that gave you hope*—you've loved every minute of it.

See the difference between the unrelieved agony story and the tension and relief pattern? You, as a spectator, will reject the all-agony story and be enthralled by the tension and relief design. Because the latter tempers torment with hope

There is another vital reason for suspense through tension and relief. When their dauntless hero has faced an early crisis and triumphed, audiences relax. They're pleased and lulled now that things are going the hero's way. Their guard is down, when *pow!*—fate belts their hero from the blind side. Dramatic shock hits them that much harder when they don't expect it.

Note how they handled it in *Earthquake*. They started with a small-scale earth tremor. Then they simmered things down for a while. Because the safer the audience feels, the more shattered it is by the next smashing shock. That is the progressive pattern for high-impact suspense.

Let me point out, at the risk of being obvious, the folly of the reverse pattern. That would be putting the major earth crunch early in the story. One great big smashing shock! Sure, you jolt the viewers half out of their seats. But then you can't top it. Instead of a rising tension, your play slides downhill. How many scores of TV films and major movies have you seen where the last half just flattens out like a leaky tire? That's called *third-act trouble*. And the sure way to avoid it is to keep a sharp eye on the Richter suspense scale and save your big smash dramatic shock for the climax.

Now that we have diagnosed suspense by definition and example, the next question is: How do you create it? There are six prime ways and means. They are:

Conflict

The commonest method of generating suspense is through conflict. Conflict usually pits the hero's high purpose against the heavy's hostility. When the script is skillfully crafted, the audience sits there glued to see who's going to win. Recall great social dramas (*In the Heat of the Night*), action-adventure tales (*High Noon*), horror stories (*Rosemary's Baby*), crime sagas (*The Godfather*), and science fiction (*Star Wars*).

But in most stories you can't settle for one-on-one conflict. A single-situation plot seems to play on a treadmill; instead of progressing, it just spins its dramatic wheels. To juice up your central situation you introduce aggravated conflicts, fresh complications. These stepped-up crises have a single purpose—to increase the suspense.

A Master Antagonist

Suspense in most stories is powered by the bad guy. A sure way to maximize that suspense is to set up a master antagonist.

This means an overwhelming adversary. Such as the evil force in *The Exorcist* or the great white shark in *Jaws*.

Of course you can't put a live shark in a soap opera, but you can replace him with a correspondingly ruthless male or female. Historic examples are the Boston Strangler, Bluebeard, or Jack the Ripper. Frankenstein's monster has terrorized more people than that white shark. In less gory dimensions were Shylock, Iago, and Lady Macbeth. Madame DeFarge in *A Tale of Two Cities* was a super-spooky lady.

Goliath, of course, was king of the club. Remember him, all pumped up to crush our little hero, David? And in those two characters lies a simple suspense secret. Give the bad guy the long bones and the heavy muscle. Doom your little hero. Because then you are dooming the audience.

Your audiences are always the good guys. The deadlier the antagonist you turn loose on them, the greater your script's suspense.

Footnote on the master antagonist. Introduce him early. Gut suspense begins at the bullfight when the bull charges into the arena to kill the matador. Open the story gates for your bull at the first logical moment. Remember—nobody ever sat there in suspense, waiting for the suspense to start.

Compounding Suspense

Here is an effective pattern in jeopardy structure, especially in action-adventure stories. I learned this years ago while writing for a youngsters' action-adventure series called "Captain Midnight."

The producer told all writers, "We have a flat rule. Get Midnight in danger early, and then keep increasing his danger to the finish."

This is a workbench technique for almost any thriller. The *Guns of Navarone* formula is a master example, which was also the "Mission: Impossible" game plan. First act: your heroes face mortal danger as they cross a hostile border. Second act: dangers double and triple as they approach enemy objective. Third act: danger goes crazy as they attack objective. Then you get them home anyway!

And if you suspect that this is just cheap movie or TV nonsense, think back to Shakespeare's plots in *Romeo and Juliet* and in *Hamlet*. Shakespeare put Romeo and Hamlet in perilous situations in the first act and then heightened that peril, scene by scene, right up to the tragic finish.

The Dreadful Alternative

Remember the *dreadful alternative* that we discussed in the opening chapter on the three-act design? Also called the *or-else factor*. It is the ghastly fate that will befall the hero if he fails to solve his story's problem. Your script offers him life or death, riches or ruin, love or loneliness. When you set up his alternatives in the first act, they create automatic suspense from then on throughout your story.

For example: the touching "or-else" of a long-forgotten TV anthology episode. A four-year-old Korean war orphan arrives in America, adopted by an American pilot and his wife. The little girl has lived as an animal, with other bereaved children, in the rubble of her bombed-out native city. Due to her horrible, war-torn infancy, she has never learned to smile. That is the story's dreadful alternative—she may have lost the human capacity. And that's her foster mother's problem—to induce her to smile. The suspense, and it is irresistible, hangs on that child's first smile of trust and love.

Look at the reverse of the coin. What happens if a story has no dreadful alternative? Example: a forgotten old fable that appeared on an anthology series emceed by Fred Astaire about a dozen years ago. Astaire also played the lead in this episode. He was a frightfully rich tycoon, who had sold out and retired. The only decisions he has to make are whether to play golf on his private course or go out on his yacht. So he's falling apart with boredom—that's the play's problem. His smart and sympathetic ex-secretary cons him into a modest business venture. The old firehorse smells the smoke of money, and before the story's over he's busier and richer than ever. It fell flat. No suspense. Because Astaire's only dreadful alternative was boredom on his yacht. Somehow the mass audience wasn't torn apart by that.

Put Your Audience in the Superior Position

Many feel that this is the most useful of all suspense techniques. But what does it mean—*the superior position?* It means letting the audience in on something that your characters don't know.

Classic usage: President Lincoln is preparing for an evening at Ford's Theatre. The audience knows that he will be assassinated by John Wilkes Booth.

The *Titanic* story has been done five times for films or

television. Why? Because the suspense hook is irresistible. The audience knows the ship is headed for the iceberg and oblivion. The passengers don't know it.

The technique is used constantly, and never grows old. Every time the script calls for a close-up of a rattlesnake coiled on the trail, and then cuts back to a frisky child skipping toward it, the writer is putting the audience in the superior position. They know something the child doesn't know. Besides, they can see that he's barefoot.

This suspense technique was described by an MGM producer with whom I wrote several films as "putting a condition" under a scene or a story. Such a *condition* can charge a placid sequence with electric vitality. A bomb under the hood can give the simple action of climbing into a car frightening significance.

Often a character condition established in the first act endows a whole story with tension. Remember Susan Hayward and her Academy Award–winning performance in *I Want to Live*. That screenplay was a true story, which had been in all the papers. From the opening scene, the audience knew she had to die in the gas chamber. Nobody went home early.

This device of letting the audience in on something the characters don't know creates what is called the *expected complication*. Put a bomb under a building, or under a sofa, and the audience expects it to explode. Give your heroine a fatal affliction, as in *Dark Victory*, and the audience knows she's pointed toward the pits.

I once met an old actor who had trouped the stick towns in tent shows, playing old-fashioned melodramas. One play featured a little tinkly music box that played the dove-like heroine's favorite tune. A heavy had loaded it with a powder charge that would blow the box and the girl apart if she lifted the lid to play the tune. Every night when she approached it with outstretched hand to lift the lid, the actor told me, some hick in the gallery would stand up and yell, "No! Stop! Don't touch it, lady. It's going to blow up."

That is the expected complication, and the history of drama is peppered with blown-up music boxes. As your scripts should be, if you hope to sell them.

The Unexpected Complication

The expected complication, just discussed, sets up protracted suspense that may endure throughout a play. This contrasts sharply with the suspense shock device, the *un*expected complication, or nasty twist. Your hero is in plenty of trouble (which, of course, he must be in any suspense structure), when something wholly unforeseen goes wrong. Now he's in four times as much trouble.

In *Romeo and Juliet*, once more for an example, Juliet is in thick soup, having secretly married Romeo of the enemy family. Her father calls her into his study and tells her he's picked out for her a guy called Paris and that she's got to marry him. *Un*expected complication for bride Juliet. Nasty twist.

Sometimes in designing your plot you have your choice between the expected complication and the unexpected. Suspense vs. surprise. Suspense thrives on expectancy, anticipation; surprise, on shock.

For example, we'll play a simple situation two ways.

First for shock. A young couple in a garden. They have just become engaged. They head for her father's study to break the news, and ask his blessing. Entering through the French windows, they find her father crumpled up on the floor. He's been stabbed with a silver letter opener, and he's dead. Dramatic shock.

Now consider the same situation written for suspense. Young couple outside in garden become engaged. Camera cuts inside to father's study. He's having a row with a heavy. The heavy stabs him with the letter opener. The killer starts out through windows to garden. Sees the young couple coming. He's got to buy time to make a getaway. He drags Papa's body to a closet, hides it, and splits.

Young couple come in. Puzzled. She was sure Papa was

there. Now you have suspense, because the audience knows he is dead in the closet, and the characters don't. They see signs of struggle. He finds the letter opener with blood on it. Dawning realization of tragedy. More suspense as they search around. She sees blood, leading to the closet. He opens it; body falls out. Ultimate dramatic shock.

There are endless arguments as to which is better—suspense or shock. Years ago I worked on a script with Tod Browning, the screen's genius of suspense in the early days. He made landmark shockers like *The Unholy Three* starring Lon Chaney. He could give you goose pimples just ad-libbing a scene at the lunch table. Anyway, he told me that there was no solution to the suspense vs. surprise dispute. Each case, he said, was special, different. The choice you make depends on the material you have in hand.

Suspense is often preferable. But remember in *Jaws* when the shark blasted into close-up through the underside of the hero's boat? That was one of the great dramatic kicks in modern movies. Because it was unexpected. And that was straight shock!

Suspense Killers
Misconstructions to Avoid

Predictability. Never let your audience get ahead of you. Writing a play is like enchanting your small child with a riddle. If he knows the answer, the fun has gone out of the game. For example, our faithful friend Hamlet. If "The Tragedy of Hamlet" were told as a newspaper story, the headline would read: KING OF DENMARK SLAIN BY PARANOID PRINCE. That headline steals the last act. It would still be a fascinating and tragic story, but a soft tire, dramatically. The suspense has leaked out of it, because your audience children know the answer.

Battle of the Sexes. In an action-adventure, a muscle drama, don't set up a woman heavy—one-on-one—against a male hero. Traditionally, action heroes are too adept, too powerful physically. An audience just won't worry about Calamity Jane riding into town to gun down Bat Masterson.

The cure for such a mismatch is to surround your shameless lady with powerful security, muscle guys who will mow down the hero if he even sneers at her.

Take further note that a heroine as legal and lethal as Angie Dickinson (in "Police Woman") is supported by an all-male police department. Any one of those boys would kill for her, and they usually do. Consider, also, the lady-in-charge in a heroine action-adventure TV series such as "The Girl from U.N.C.L.E." She comes complete with a macho sidekick to take care of all important bloodletting.

This has nothing to do with male chauvinism. Movie audiences are aware that Muhammad Ali could pulverize any woman that ever lived with one hand tied behind him. To disregard this in an action drama is simply to erode your suspense.

Odds Against Your Hero. Take care that you do not set up a too powerful hero. If your Noble Hunter has the loudest horns and all the horses, his clash with the villain Fox won't generate much suspense. Besides, audiences are balky; sympathy may go out to that little scared Fox. Your effective technique is to reverse the situation. Load the odds *against* your good guy. The less chance he has, the harder the audience will sweat for him.

The Last Ditch. Never wipe out your major villain before the finish. If he personifies the power of evil threatening your hero, he must keep riding to the climax. When the presiding bad guy dies too early, the rest will be *anti*climax.

How many times have you seen a western with the cowboys and the outlaws in a pitched battle finish? The boss outlaw chickens out, and rides off down the canyon. But the hero has seen him, and follows. He corners and kills him, *one-on-one.* And the message of this is:

To keep suspense alive, your villain always dies in the last ditch.

Suspense Wears Two Hats

Suspense in your script never quits, if you wind it up tight and start it off properly. You can even make it work for you on two story levels at the same time.

1. Overall Suspense. In the first act you introduce your top dog (hero), his opponent (bad dog), and the bone they are fighting over (problem). This conflict sets up instant suspense. You nourish this with complications, which increase your rising tension to the climax. Thus you create a beginning-to-end suspense, which is the emotional backbone of your entire dramatic structure.
2. Miniature Tension Pattern in Major Scenes. If you put a magnifying glass on great individual scenes in drama, you'll often find they have a beginning, a middle, and an end of their own.

For the evidence, let's return to *Romeo and Juliet.* We'll take the balcony scene as our illustration. To most people that scene is solely an outpouring of the most radiant love lyrics ever written. But let's take a clinical look at it.

Romeo, having fallen in love with Juliet at the ball, comes to her balcony that night. His problem is Everyman's and hers is Everywoman's. Each is in love, each has got to find out how the other feels about it. Suspense. She appears on the balcony. She doesn't know that Romeo's down below, but the audience can see him there. Thus more suspense. She confesses her love to the starry night. Romeo hears her. Partial relief!

Now Romeo steps out of the shadows and declares his love for her.

Mutual enchantment. Total relief from tension But into

the next moment intrudes anxiety, new suspense. Because of her family's rancor, Juliet fears for his life.

But they decide their love transcends tribal hatreds. She declares she will marry him anyway! New problems—how, where, when? Juliet says she'll send her messenger next morning to set the time and place. She's called inside by her nurse. Scene climaxes on highest expectation, deepest anxiety. Marriage may both fulfill and destroy them.

Thus, an important scene, in the hands of an instinctive craftsman, becomes a miniature drama in itself. Shakespeare told his love story in a sequence of such suspenseful scenes. And *in resolving each crisis, he created another!* Thus, the progressive tension increased until the play's resolution, which was the lovers' reunion in death.

Milking a Suspense Situation

Milking, a common term in the trade, means squeezing the maximum dramatic effect out of any given situation or scene.

The practice seems so obvious, why do we bother? Because even veteran writers sometimes squander their suspense resources. Beginners characteristically do.

To illustrate, we're going to take a couple of dizzying jumps from *Romeo and Juliet* to "I Love Lucy," and then to the Swedish genius, Ingmar Bergman.

Crack comedy writers are among the finest craftsmen in Hollywood. This scene is from an outstanding TV special Lucy and Desi did with Danny Thomas.

Lucy and Desi have rented Danny's mansion for the season, but they have found it is haunted or full of bedbugs or something—and they want out of their lease. But Desi has given Danny their check. If he cashes it, they're stuck with the house. Lucy knows that Danny has secreted the check in the drawer of his night table and that he is a late sleeper.

Early the next morning she sneaks into his bedroom to retrieve the check. Basic comedy suspense—virtuous housewife in a strange male's bedroom. Lucy reconnoiters, sees Danny asleep. Tension.

She tiptoes directly to the night table and finds the check. She's safe! Big relief. Note that she could have walked straight out and ended the scene. But they milked it.

Lucy starts out, past a big wilting plant. She can't resist watering it. She spills some water, has to wipe it up, makes some noise. Danny half wakes up. He thinks she's his wife, who we know has left in the car for town. He says groggily, "Come here."

Lucy ducks into the nearest door, which is the bathroom. There she puts on the wife's muu-muu for disguise, reappears and starts to tiptoe past the bed. He's apparently back to sleep. But just as she passes, he reaches out and whacks her on the fanny. Lucy shudders and freezes.

Now Danny demands that his "wife" scratch his back. Forces her to sit on the bed. See how they're milking it, topping themselves every time. At this point of no return, they bring back his real wife. She's forgotten her car keys—and the whole scene goes up in smoke.

Note, incidentally, that this scene is designed like a miniature play: problem, complication, climax. And if any of you feel that it's primary, I had a student who recently caught the episode on the afternoon reruns. She reported that now, fifteen or twenty years later, it was still hilarious!

This technique of milking a suspense situation is so essential that we will examine a classic dramatic example, Ingmar Bergman's *Virgin Spring*. Bergman, of course, is enshrined by many among the greatest moviemakers, living or dead.

In *The Virgin Spring* Bergman dramatized a legend from the Middle Ages. In the first act the virgin daughter of a noble landowner sets out on horseback Sunday morning to take a gift of votive candles to the district church. She's accompanied by a pregnant, half-crazy peasant girl whom the family has befriended. They are waylaid by two roving herdsmen and their little brother. The pregnant girl escapes, but the herdsmen rape and murder the virgin daughter.

Traveling on, the herdsmen come to the estate of the landowner. Not knowing that this was the murdered girl's home, they ask for a night's lodging and are made welcome.

Thus is established a major suspense situation. Murderers of the family's cherished daughter are overnight guests in the family house. What supplies the suspense? The audience is in a superior position. They know what the film's characters don't know. They have seen the rape and murder. They are anticipating the obligatory scene—the discovery by the girl's father that his daughter is dead and that these men killed her.

Bergman played that one situation for the rest of the picture—except for a brief tag. About an hour of film. That's why we are focusing on it—because it is a landmark example of getting the most out of a strong situation. The family gathers for dinner. The kid brother of the killers is in psychic shock from witnessing the murder. He gets sick and has to be taken to bed.

Next morning one of the killers figures he can make travel money by selling to the mother some rich garments from the murdered girl. Mother recognizes them. Doesn't blow it open. Goes to father. Tension rises as suspicion begins to crystallize. Then the crazy pregnant servant girl gets back. She's seen the murder and identifies the killers. But still no dramatic explosion.

Notice how Bergman is spacing it out—getting every last ounce out of a heavy suspense situation. Now the father is convinced. He calls a farmhand for his slaughtering knife (with which he killed cattle). Armed with the knife, he finally faces the murderers—about an hour of screen time after the suspense situation was established. In a gory scene, he kills them.

Note that this same confrontation scene could have been told in perhaps ten minutes. For example: the killers arrive, are offered dinner and a night's lodging. But the mad servant girl returns. She accuses them. The daughter's clothes are found in their pack. Her father, convinced by this evidence, wipes them out. That would have made a tense, chilling sequence, but how wasteful. From the same raw materials Bergman spun an hour or more of magic—most of the second and third acts of his striking drama.

These examples suggest a conscious creative process when you are working out your screenplay.

Evaluate each scene. If it is of lesser importance, it's often better to underplay and accelerate it. Give it a single punch and send it on its way.

But when you come to a major scene, exploit it for maximum values. Structure it, if possible, with a beginning, a middle, and an end. Then squeeze the suspense for the last cold bead of audience sweat.

Looking Back—Wrapping Up

Drama is the essence of a human experience. But the characters and events are not just cataloged as in a computer readout. Nor are you, the dramatist, just any guy in a bar trading anecdotes, or a housewife gabbing over her back fence.

You are a magician in the spotlight of a darkened theater. You have at your command an infinite treasure of story illusions. All the children in the world are sitting out there in front of you, because the name of your act is "Suspense."

For those children you are not just telling a story. You are binding a spell!

5.

CONTENT AND EMOTION

The Heart Has a Mind of Its Own.

Content and emotion in the same dramatic story may seem a strange mix, since content is a kind of brain marrow, while emotion floods up from the glands.

Yet the record shows that this odd couple produces distinguished offspring—plays for the stage, screen, or television which explore truth. They are *about something*. At the same time they earn landmark cash profits.

During this discussion some years ago, a student couldn't wait to get his hand up and disagree heatedly. He named a TV and film producer who had told him flatly that "message" stories were out. The producer said he wouldn't buy that kind of heavy stuff for his program, because he knew that the only thing that sold tickets was *entertainment!*

This was an enshrined belief throughout the early California movie industry. Most of you have heard the gag they coined about it back in the Thirties. The classic, cigar-chomping studio boss shouting at the mousey writer: "If you've got a message, kid, take it to Western Union."

The modern producer our student quoted about entertainment simply revealed how ignorant he was about the history of his own trade. Big movies of forty years ago often had important things to say.

Film buffs recognize ancient giants with vital themes: *The Informer, The Story of Louis Pasteur, The Lost Weekend, Boys' Town, All Quiet on the Western Front.*

Let's belabor the obvious by skipping straight to the Seventies. And let's forget million-dollar movies for the moment and zoom in on commercial television.

In the TV season of 1975 David Gerber, then executive producer at Columbia Studios Television, addressed his assembled executives and salesmen. He spoke of television as the moral force of show business. He cited *A Case of Rape, The Autobiography of Miss Jane Pittman,* and other significant dramas of that season. He said television could treat serious social problems that theatrical films couldn't touch.

Perhaps this was a little exaggerated, since major films had been treating social problems for thirty years before TV ever started, and live theater had been doing it some twenty-five centuries before that.

But there it is. Even television tycoons—traditionally cautious—are spreading the "message" message. And more and more of their flagship projects are based on the conflict between good and ill in the human heart and throughout our society. In short, their money films have ethical and moral points to make. They are *about something.*

Think back not only on the big TV specials, but on many of the great television series.

Remember "The Defenders," from which all of today's lawyer shows draw their inspiration. That legal team—father and son—was selling only one staple: human justice.

Remember "The Fugitive," one of the longest running of the dramatic series. Week after week, for all those years, it made a statement: a good doctor values the life of a sick person above his own.

Think of the homely virtues of "The Waltons," for several

years the top-rated drama on the air—except perhaps for "All in the Family," in which Archie Bunker draws a scathing cartoon every week of a gassy conservative. "M*A*S*H" satirizes the stupid military. Almost every police show enshrines the honest cop. Thus—week by week—virtually all the leading dramatic shows put positive points on the board.

But quickly let me caution you against announcing to a producer—as part of your sales pitch—that your script has a message. Never! The old taboo against "message" films still haunts executive offices. Say instead, "It makes a statement."

And don't laugh when you say it. This is not a gag, but standard coinage for professionals. *Statement* is the in-word. Producers and networks are royally skilled at double-entry bookkeeping. They have found that the moral statement of a fine script can be powerfully reflected in its profit statement.

All professional writers, however, know that the diehard producer who scorned message stories was right in one respect. Stuffy sermon plays can be slow death. Audiences will not sit still for a writer who scolds or lectures them from a soapbox. None of us will.

Don't worry. No problem. Just stay out of the pulpit. Address your audience on ground level, like a baseball field, or a ghetto street, or a *Shampoo*-type cocktail party. A bum vomiting his life away in a gutter will concern more people about alcoholism than a bishop preaching in the local cathedral.

Develop your moral content so skillfully that they don't suspect you. Some examples: *My Fair Lady* and *The King and I*, among the biggest musical hits in stage history—both entertainments with content. *West Side Story*, which is still running in movie theaters around the world, had a clear statement to make: he who lives by violence, will die by violence. *Lady Sings the Blues* was a drug evil story. *Cabaret* was an anti-Nazi diatribe. Note that I've chosen five *musicals* to illustrate the point, because musicals suggest comics and chorus lines. I also checked the list of Academy Oscar nominees for Best Picture of many years. In the entire list almost none were solely entertainment projects. And the classic films that made enduring statements included the following.

All Quiet on the Western Front. (The first great antiwar picture.)

Mutiny on the Bounty. (An exposé of the inhuman cruelty of the British Maritime laws.)

The Lost Weekend. (The first film drama about alcoholism.)

Gentlemen's Agreement. (The first film exposé of American anti-Semitism.)

On the Waterfront. (A revelation of labor union racketeering.)

A Man for All Seasons. (A man willing to die for his faith.)

In the Heat of the Night. (A play about bigotry and racism.)

Midnight Cowboy. (A drama about friendship and loyalty.)

One Flew over the Cuckoo's Nest. (An exposé of conditions in our mental institutions.)

All the President's Men. (You all know what that was about.)

With memorable productions such as those, we are dealing with super scripts, big budgets, and star personalities. Again, let's cut the design way down to unpretentious weekly television. Perhaps an hour episode of "Kojak."

Somebody kills somebody. We witness that. But why? Because that somebody stands in the way of a desire or an ambition. The killer thus sacrifices his higher instinct to satisfy a baser instinct. He is, therefore, ruthless. Kojak appears and starts to harass him. To maintain his advantage the killer has to knock off someone else. But now his own web begins to close in around him. He is cornered by Kojak and caught. The statement made by this typical exercise is: the killer's final victim is himself. But this is the theme of countless classic dramas and smash movie successes—*Macbeth*, *West Side Story*, *Little Caesar*, *Bonnie and Clyde*.

Defining Content

Incidentally, *content* is kind of a hazy word. It has many other names: *theme, premise, substance, text,* or *thesis.* But they all end up meaning one thing. They define the ethical or moral point of your story. Incidentally, are you damn sure that you know it? Because, if you don't, the audience won't have a clue.

When the curtain falls, or the film fades out, the audience for a fine play hopes to leave your presence with a feeling of clearer wisdom, perhaps rage, or even exaltation. But not confusion.

The most destructive comment in any lobby or living room is: "Now what the hell was that all about?"

To avoid that embarrassing question, there is a foolproof technique. Lajos Egri propounds it in the opening chapter of his thoughtful book, *The Art of Dramatic Writing.* He suggests, nay insists, that you boil down your play's meaning into a single sentence. Because a good play is usually a human experience that illustrates a principle. The single sentence expresses that principle. Some examples follow.

Othello: "Jealousy consumes a man and destroys the one he loves."

A Doll's House, by Ibsen, the first of the women's lib stories in modern drama: "A wife treated as a toy will revolt as a human being."

"The Fugitive,' TV series; and *The Hospital,* Academy Award–winning screenplay: "A doctor's duty to his patients transcends his personal concerns and comforts."

Romeo and Juliet: "A family feud will destroy the brightest and best of both houses."

Macbeth: "Ruthless ambition drives men, and women, too, to their own destruction."

The Treasure of the Sierra Madre: "Greed will consume those who practice it."

Content is also a cornerstone of enduring comedy. An example, already cited: *My Fair Lady,* adapted from George

Bernard Shaw's *Pygmalion*. It not only ridicules British social snobbery generally, but also says specifically: "No one should exploit another person for his selfish, intellectual ends."

Incidentally, Shaw, certainly among the greatest of English authors, knew the dangers of preaching in the theater. And among his many comments about the dramatist's task was this: "If you're going to tell people the truth, you'd better make them laugh—or they'll kill you."

At about this point in our discussion of content, a technical question often arises:

"Do you express your play's premise in words in your script? If so, when and where do you verbalize it?"

The answer is: "You don't." Rarely, if ever, do we find the content or meaning spelled out in a line of dialogue. A fine play makes a moral point in terms of a human experience. But no audience wants that moral rammed down its throat, like the text of a sermon on Sunday.

Let me give you a horrible exception to prove the rule. A weekly TV action series was winding up the week's shooting, when it found itself several minutes short. That is disaster time. If you're long, you can always clip some scenes out. But if you're short, you can't just roll blank film. So the producer and director hastily wrote a tag, which consisted mostly of a lonely soliloquy by the old character actor, their guest star. He was a great old ham, and went right into it with gusto. But halfway through he blew his lines. He fixed the camera with a sagacious eye and ad-libbed, word by cliché word, the story's moral platitude. It was the last take of the day. The sun went down and they had to leave it in. And the story editor told me later, with a kind of professional nausea: "Do you know that we got more favorable mail on that speech than on any one bit so far in the whole goddamn series."

But that's the *exception!* The virtually unbreakable rule is *not* to verbalize your premise. Just be very sure that *you* are aware of it. I've known writers who sweated out one-sentence meanings of their scripts, and tacked them or the wall in front of them. It helps to know, even in a cop show, that there is something worthwhile being said beneath all your required crime and chase sequences.

There's still another way of describing content. It should combine a cause with an effect. A lot of modern short fiction and many avant-garde plays offer mood pieces, portraits of people not going anywhere. Often beautifully written, they offer only emotion that flares up and is gone. This is flashbulb writing. Lacking is the *effect* of that emotion.

On the big screen, or the square tube, I believe an audience wants more than a flame shining briefly in darkness. They want it to shine for a man or a woman in conflict, danger, or despair. As a warning against invasion, or as a beacon of hope. And above all, they want your protagonist to *do* something about it. Which is to say that a play should concern its audience with a cause, and pay them off with an effect.

Let's check out content in that most important of all dramatic plot lines—the character-change story. This is the self-knowledge plot structure, in which your protagonist faces a tragic flaw in his nature and does something positive about it. Thus you dramatize content through human experience. I do not care whether or not you can state your play's point in a copybook maxim. If you can raise your central character from despair and delusion to higher ground of truth and self-belief, then you have told the universal story of personal evolution, and your play has content.

But there is something else. No professional writer could end this section without a personal note to all those coming up behind him.

If your script is a mechanical project, or a vaudeville turn with mostly pratfalls—in short, if it has no meaning, premise, content, call it what you like—then getting it down on paper can be grueling work. Nothing is so difficult as the meaningless scene, forced on you by a gimmicky plot line. When your whole story is pointless, no matter how clever and salable, then for a week or two your typewriter grinds like a dentist's drill.

But if you've got a true comedy with satiric overtones, or a basic drama with a theme that really says something—that is one of writing's greatest rewards.

The best TV show I ever wrote was "The Charlatan" for the General Electric Theatre—about a cancer quack. I felt deeply about it. I had a brother-in-law who was a tumor specialist, and he had told me about the murders by slow torture such men commit. I had a play with a premise, something I could take sides on. I had an emotion I could transmit to an audience. It was one of the easiest-to-write scripts I ever did. It took me just a week, and was shot, almost intact, as written.

When you get one like that—a story that you feel and believe in—then writing it can be a rare kind of pleasure. It is like climbing a difficult mountain, just for the thrill of getting to the top. Or running after a fire engine when you were twelve years old. Nothing is work when you're having such a hell of a good time doing it.

You are having such a good time, I suggest, because you believe in those scenes you are writing. And you had better believe in them! If a writer's work is to live beyond broadcast night, he had better be outraged, or inspired, or sick to his stomach about something.

If you need any added proof, remember some of the great ones in television: *My Sweet Charlie*, *A Christmas Story*, *Brian's Song*, *The Missiles of October*, "Roots," and *Scared Straight*. Compare them with many samples of weekly series comedies and dramas, and you'll see why television has been called a eunuch art. Because the grind shows too often have the empties. They live on *craftsmanship without conviction*.

And finally let me remind you that you do not have to have a new and original premise. There probably isn't any such thing. Your story can have a racial theme; it can condemn government corruption or expose hustling. Just be sure it says *something*—something that a theater full of people will accept as valid and worth hearing.

How many great antiwar plays and films have you seen,

and will you continue to see until war is laid to its last bloody resting place? Virtually all of them say exactly the same thing.

"Applause," said Ambrose Bierce, "is the echo of a platitude." Only that's not a funny; and do you know why? *Because there is no such thing as cliché truth.*

Emotion

"Drama is concerned only with emotion." This dictum comes from Paddy Chayefsky, who has won more Academy Awards for his original scripts that any other film writer. "Your basic story," he concludes, "is also the emotional line of your script."

The reasons for this are wholly practical. By engaging your spectators' emotions, you give them the illusion that they are sharing the dramatic experience. And that illusion, above all else, is what they spend their hard-won wages for when they flock nightly to the world's movie theaters. As usual, let's cut to examples.

As You Like It. Love is the central emotion; the obvious primitive and universal appeal. Every audience identifies with lovers. Will they or won't they win each other in the end? *Love Story*, which made a great many million dollars, is another certified copy.

Jaws, *Earthquake*, and the disaster cycle. Human survival is the emotion, and that's as basic as you can get.

The Sound of Music. This combined love *and* survival, if you recall. Would Julie Andrews win the man she loved, and later would they escape from the Nazis and Austria? There was a lot of warm laughter along the way. The film was—in dollar terms—among the most successful ever made.

One Flew over the Cuckoo's Nest. The emotion was fear and horror. The star, Jack Nicholson, was crazy and sane at the same time. And since all of us are a little like that, it won five Academy Awards.

A Case of Rape. One of the highest-rated movies ever made for television. The emotion was terror—through identification with Elizabeth Montgomery as the rape victim. In the all-time TV champion, "Roots," the emotion was the horror and humiliation of human slavery.

This is a tiny handful of examples. If you care to check, there are literally thousands of others—plays and films that won worldwide audiences because they aroused primal emotions . . . emotions which the customers in the seats could share with their other selves in the play.

If you do not set up this current of emotion between screen and spectator, then he's just following you with his eyes and ears—objectively, but without the gut empathy. Beware of a spectator when he just sits there thinking about what you've written. He may think to switch you off, and go to "Laverne & Shirley" or "All in the Family."

A certain wise writer put it like this: "You need skill to create conflict and suspense, but it takes talent to make an audience care."

Yet that's your key task: to create people in crisis with whom the audience can identify *emotionally.* To the point that they feel they have a personal stake in the way your play turns out.

A few pages back I quoted Paddy Chayefsky: "Drama is concerned only with emotion." Frank Capra, one of the great directors, said, "The *whole thing* is—you've got to make them care about somebody."

They were both saying, in effect, the same thing.

But there's another reason—also deeply important—to arouse emotion if you wish to write for wide audiences. As we suggested earlier, a work of quality has content. The writer has a statement to make on a human issue. He has taken sides.

Perhaps—as in *Death of a Salesman*—the writer wants to warn people not to pin their dreams on the cruel hypocrisy of modern business.

Perhaps—as in *A Man for All Seasons*—the writer wants to inspire people with the example of a man who was willing to die for his beliefs.

Perhaps—as in *Hustling*—the writer wants to expose the barbarity of big-city prostitution.

In brief, the writer has a point to make. But we've already agreed that you can't preach a sermon. People hate sermon plays, and they just won't buy tickets.

Therefore, you strive for a combined effect. Audiences watch films with their glands. If you can get them worked up emotionally, they'll not only absorb your statement, they'll bug their friends to run down and catch the film.

On the contrary, if your scenes have no emotional charge, they'll get bored. And stop listening. By next week all their friends will have been warned *not* to buy tickets. And you'll be preaching to an empty church.

A famous New York stage producer of the Roaring Twenties, Arthur Hopkins, put it this way in a cogent but now little-known book about playwriting called *How's Your Second Act?*:

"I do not want the emotion that arises out of thought, but thought that arises out of emotion."

In brief, you must arouse the emotions of people, old and young, to induce them to think. It has been said that the function of many a fine play is to stir up the bad conscience of society. Because most people—including thee and me—have closed minds in certain areas We perhaps sum it up with the gag of the old diehard: "I know what's right and what's wrong on this subject—so don't bother me with the facts."

A good play or film is a device to bother people with the facts.

In a classroom discussion of these matters, a student waved his hand at this point to say something. He told us that he worked in some aspect of law enforcement for the Los Angeles city government. He said that the television special *A Case of Rape*, starring Elizabeth Montgomery, had so stirred up City Hall and the population that it had already affected police handling of rape cases. That television show, exposing an evil injustice, had actually introduced a new humanity in police stations and courtrooms where rape victims appeared. In many states these new attitudes are being defined by law. In simpler words—the process works. This is because the only knowledge that counts on stage or screen is *felt knowledge*. We learn through feeling.

James Stephens, Irish poet and novelist, expressed it in general terms better than any writer I know:

"I have learned that the head does not feel anything until the heart has listened. And what the heart knows today, the head will understand tomorrow."

6.

BEGINNING YOUR SCREENPLAY

The question of how to begin your dramatic story is rarely raised in our UCLA class. Nor perhaps, is it raised often enough in some film producers' offices. Probably because the answer seems so obvious.

You should begin, of course, at the beginning. Introduce your characters; sketch in your story background.

No. Wrong! That's the Gaslight Theater gospel from way back before movies even existed. The modern answer is: begin with flying saucers, a murder, or two couples in bed, followed by a ski chase (as in *The Spy Who Loved Me*).

A memorable example is the great white shark in *Jaws*. Remember how early in that screenplay the shark chewed up its first screaming bather? Then, and not until then, did the writers develop the characters and the background of their New England summer resort.

Jaws was a primitive melodrama, to be sure. It was also the highest grossing film in theatrical history until *Star Wars* came along. Writers and employers of writers will dismiss its audience-appeal technique at some risk. Especially when we find that technique repeated in modern film after successful film. And not just suspense and fury films either. *All the President's Men* did not start with biographies of Woodward, Bern-

stein, and Richard Nixon. It opened with the Watergate burglary.

A classic example of this technique is the murder mystery.
Drama begins with violent or inscrutable death. Then Ellery
Queen or Sherlock Holmes or Columbo appears to stalk the
murderer.

The detective investigates the beginnings of the story. As
he digs out clues and discovers motives, he fills the audience in
on indispensable background. Who was the dead man? Why
should someone want to kill him? Was it a grudge death or
blackmail or greed? Thus the writer briefs his audience on the
back story. The back story concerns who did what to whom
before the film started—the people, the emotions, the broken
commandments that led to homicide.

Such exposition, or back story, is a must in most plots to
educate the audience as to what the hell is going on. But its
handling can be the bane of beginning writers. And every so
often, of experienced screenwriters, too. They forget that audiences did not pay to be educated about what happened five
years, or five hours, before the film started. They're engrossed
in what's happening before their eyes. Which of those carefree
bathers is the shark going to feed on next?

Let's make things nauseatingly clear by busing everybody
back to an opening night at a Broadway theater in the Gay
Nineties. The curtain rises on the breakfast room of an English
manor house. Starchy butler and gushy maid are polishing the
silver for a gala dinner that evening. The only son is returning
from building bridges in Northern Karoo.

MAID
It's jolly good that the young master comes
home rich and successful.

BUTLER
Don't be gossiping, Nessie. Tend to your
work. Whatever makes you say that?

                        MAID
Ha, Meekins ... we all know that the old
Earl, his father, has lost his fortune to the
card gamblers.

                        BUTLER
                    (wistfully)
And the disgrace has driven her dear old
Ladyship to drink and delirium tremens.

                        MAID
But saddest of all, the blue-eyed angel the
young master loved as a girl has eloped
with that dim-witted butcher.

At this point carriage wheels are heard on the drive, and the returning hero bounds on stage to begin the drama.

In this way gifted playwrights briefed the customers on vital statistics needed to understand the plot. They dared do this because they had *captive audiences*. All those people out front in high collars and corsets had paid cash at the wicket. Nobody was going to budge, at least until the curtain fell on the first act.

Jump cut sixty years later. The theater and even the prosperous film industry face a rowdy upstart called television. Captive audiences have been replaced by fifty million escapists. They sit hunched in front of their sets hoping to escape their troubles.

Writers who bore them with dull first acts are trouble they do not need. They escape, with a spin of the dial, to John Travolta, or the lady wrestling matches. Such defections the networks cannot allow. Without those escapist millions watching commercials, television programs self-destruct.

Thus the smash beginning became a mandate. The most powerful art form in human history was structured to accommodate hucksters of tobacco products, motor vehicles, and packaged cheese.

This is not to say that great dramatic stories never before

had crisis openings. Many did, and we will specify some in a few moments. But television made the crash beginning obligatory, and the technique soon infiltrated wide-screen theatrical films.

Sometimes whole scenes are played even before the credit titles flood the screen.

Let it be quickly noted that certain filmmakers reject this technique. Some significant films still begin with leisurely character and atmospheric exposition. The award-winning *Julia* was one of them. But the crisis beginning is such a high percentage that a practical screenwriter will come to terms with it. He will discover, as he designs his first act, that he has three broad choices.

The Action Opening

We place this first only because it serves writers so incessantly in both TV and films. Murder is the classic. Kidnappings, train wrecks, holdups, car crashes are routine variations. Recall—for one familiar example—*The Godfather Part II*, which opens with a succession of murders in Sicily. (And it went on to earn one of the biggest grosses in world entertainment history.)

Situation Opening

To illustrate this for my UCLA class I chose a long-forgotten episode from the Alfred Hitchcock anthology series. (I had found that constant reference to the classics and box-office recordbreakers could intimidate inexperienced students. It was like matching their fledgling melodies against those of Gershwin or Beethoven.)

The scene is a British rubber plantation in Malaysia. The day's work over, one of the owners is mixing a pink gin. He is summoned by a panicked cry from his partner. Dashing to a bedroom, he discovers the latter lying on his bed under a sheet.

While his partner was asleep, a deadly viper had crawled

into bed. The snake now lies comfortably curled up on the Englishman's stomach, taking a little nap of its own.

If the man moves, the snake will bite. Its venom is fatal. He pleads for his partner to do something! Nobody switched off that TV episode until the partner got the snake off his stomach.

The Character Hook

This is probably the most rewarding of the attention winners. It presents an engaging or compelling individual facing a character crisis. Neil Simon used it in a delightful romantic comedy. In his very first scene, the heroine comes home to her New York apartment to find that her lover has split for keeps. It's happened before. She's a girl whom males walk out on. That's what the film is about, and why Simon called it *The Good-bye Girl*.

If this seems a fluffy sample, recall the character hook that George Bernard Shaw used to begin *Pygmalion*. Shaw introduced a Cockney flower girl, Liza Doolittle, and the pompous Professor Higgins. Higgins proposed to transform ignorant Liza into a high-bred London lady. Audiences in the millions settled back happily to watch her exaltation.

Perhaps greatest of all such character openings is in the story of Joan of Arc. God proposes to transform an ignorant peasant girl into the military savior of France. World audiences haven't been able to switch that one off for hundreds of years.

Very well, you have devised a crisis opening that hooks your audience. Now can you slow down and establish your back story? Not often, you can't. Most plots don't have a shark swimming around to keep everyone on red alert.

Yet you must provide background briefing; who's done what to whom, and when, where, and why? Such statistics are boring; first acts cannot be. How do you reconcile these opposites?

You rely, in most stories, on four major techniques, and two minor.

Conflict

Conflict heads the list. The dullest exposition scene will divert an audience if the characters start dumping on each other. Their crossfire can be refined or gutbucket. Words are weapons. As characters belabor each other, audiences happily absorb plot points. Our earlier discussion on conflict (see Chapter 3) contains more on this, with specific examples. But for television addicts, let's recall almost any police or doctor series.

Conflict scenes pit the young hero cop or intern against the crusty old police captain, or hospital chief of staff. As they wrangle, they educate the audience on police or medical essentials

Dr. Casey was the landmark example. He wasn't short-tempered and sharp-tongued just to create a character. The writers needed those yelling scenes to help them dramatize their medical case histories. Can you imagine how dull and incomprehensible they would have been if the doctors had behaved sensibly?

Suspense

The best illustration of this technique I know was quoted to me from Howard Lindsay and Russel Crouse, authors of *State of the Union* and *Life with Father*. A friend of mine asked them what they would favor as the best way to begin a dramatic story. They said they had considered the matter carefully. In their ideal opening the curtain rises on a conventional living-room setting. No actors on stage. A male nobody appears carrying a box marked DYNAMITE. He places it carefully under a center-stage sofa. Lighting the fuse, he pushes the box gently out of sight. Then he disappears backstage where he came from. After a moment, the characters in the play enter the living room and launch into their opening dialogue. Nobody in that audience could stir until that dynamite had been discovered and dealt with.

The example, however elementary, is directly to the point.

The box of dynamite is the shark in *Jaws*. As we discussed in Chapter 4, "Suspense," audiences will listen breathlessly while you stuff them with plot points—*if* you have set up a suspense condition under the scene.

Let me offer an actual example from a TV movie of the week. A man, fatally injured in a car crash, is rushed to a hospital. Dying, he makes his heart available to anyone who needs it for survival. But there are *two* patients in cardiac care, both waiting for the first heart that may be available. The doctors are faced with the godly decision. Every dramatic aspect of the two patients' lives was discussed in detail, mostly in flashbacks. Every scene and every word was back story, and yet it was all intensely vivid and effective. Because the writer had lighted a suspense fuse under the first-act crisis. Which of the two dying men, each worthy and deserving, should live, and which should die?

Humor

This method of educating audiences on back story is kin to a teaching technique of progressive schools. The little monsters don't want to be educated; but if you divert them sufficiently, they will embrace the learning process. Movie audiences are children in an eternal wonderland. They laugh, they cry, at simple stimuli. Give them an exposition scene with enough solid laughs, and they will happily soak up all your vital statistics.

Flashback

A flashback, of course, is a dip into the past, to illuminate the present dramatic situation. And if you flash back to Hollywood in the Thirties, you'll find that screenwriters were often barred from using them. Unskilled producers warned the writer help darkly that a flashback was unreal; it destroyed the mood and stopped the story flow.

Some pagan Europeans, who didn't know any better, used them anyway. Sometimes on two or three time levels. Remember *A Man and a Woman* from France; and *Two for the Road*, with Audrey Hepburn and Albert Finney, from England. Box-office profits for such films restored flashbacks to Hollywood favor. *Julia*, a 1978 success, which received eleven Academy Award nominations, was presented on several shifting time levels.

When using flashbacks, however, there is a hazard that must be respected. They can be vignettes, conflicts, comedy trips, mayhem, or death scenes. But they should *not* be just old conversations, revived to inform your audience.

A flashback should make a valid contribution of its own. It must interest or entertain.

No Exposition Needed (Rare)

Once in hundreds of first acts you will need no exposition. The drama just fires off before your eyes. *Heaven Knows, Mr. Allison*, a war film starring Robert Mitchum and Deborah Kerr, comes to mind. It opens, before the titles, on a lovely South Sea Island beach. Breaking waves are nudging a battered Navy dory to shore. The dory grounds, and a half-dead U.S. Marine crawls out. As he surveys the beach, camera pans to a figure approaching. A female figure. Deborah Kerr. She wears the black habit of a nun.

That was it. Mitchum's beat-up battle dress and Kerr's black robe were all the back story any writer ever needed.

The Hamlet Method (Rarest)

Remember the opening scene in the world's greatest play. The ghost of Hamlet's father appears on the misty battlements to lodge some indignant complaints. How he had been murdered by Hamlet's uncle, who then stole the throne of Denmark and even married Hamlet's mother. That was probably the prime deadweight exposition ever hung on the front end of a great play. How did Shakespeare do it? How did he dare?

He just reached back and called on his genius for a little extra. His time was midnight, his scene the misty battlements. He summoned his ghost from another world. The scene was so spooked-up that spectators for centuries have listened hypnotized. Of course, the poetry wasn't bad, either. In these technical matters, it helps to be Shakespeare.

Wrap-up

Opening your script with plodding back story is the mark of an amateur and the millstone of the careless professional!

Dreariest of all is the scene where a couple of characters sit down over coffee and Danish and just inform each other—and the audience—of what went down before the play started. Somebody has called this *sewing-circle dialogue*, and it can embalm your first act.

Yet exposition is required in most plots to validate the dramatic structure. You must educate your audience—fill in on character relationships and vital story points.

Therefore, your high percentage ploy is to begin in crisis. You have, broadly speaking, three choices.

An Action Crisis. Snare audience attention with a murder, a shark, or a terrorist bomb.

A Situation Crisis. A woman is raped and learns that neither the police nor the law are on her side. This was *A Case of Rape*, starring Elizabeth Montgomery.

A Character Crisis—perhaps the best. Introduce a protagonist with a strong individual interest hook—such as Jack Nicholson in the Academy Award–winning *One Flew over the Cuckoo's Nest*. Nicholson, a seemingly lucid man, is committed to an insane asylum. Or the TV news commentator in *Network*, who proposed to commit suicide on camera because his program faced cancellation.

Then, as your play develops, slip in the back story unobtrusively. To beguile your audience while doing so, call on comedy, flashbacks, and especially minor suspense and conflict scenes. Meanwhile, maintain your story flow.

Do this skillfully, and audiences will absorb your exposition as part of the story experience. They will never even notice you are cramming them. *That* is the effect you are after.

ENDING A DRAMATIC STORY

A great dramatic story has been likened to the act of love. It is the unique and moving expression of a universal experience. In both, the transcendental moments are called the *climax*.

Your finishing sequence, accordingly, is by all odds the critical area of the film-writing process. It consummates the creative response in the minds and hearts of the audience. Nor is this true only of great scripts. Even a minor dramatic story can be transformed by a memorable third act.

By reverse token, forceful ideas and compelling characters are wiped out every season by screenwriting's most mischievous ill. It is called *third-act trouble*.

Fortunately, there is preventive medicine for third-act trouble. It lies in recognizing your third act as the ultimate enemy. He is waiting around the last bend to kill you. Never kid yourself that you will easily find the idea to wipe him out when you get there. Of course, maybe you will; most of us get that lucky about one time in ten. But, perversely, we also find that certain strong dramatic situations simply have no solution.

Your best strategy, therefore, is to make your last act one of your first steps. Figure out in outline form your full three-act structure. Decide just what you are trying to say, and just where your plot line is going. Select the substance of your ending before you start writing the script.

In the broadest sense, you will have two choices in all but exceptional stories. They are the affirmative ending, and the negative. Master tragedy is a cornerstone of enduring drama, and we will discuss it presently. But the positive, or affirmative, ending is by far the high percentage choice in mass audience films and television.

This is not a matter of artistic preference—mine or yours—but a simple statement of fact. It is borne out by the box-office figures of countless films, headed by the soaring grosses of *Star Wars* and *Jaws*. Their profit totals mean that they summoned the greatest audiences, the most bodies, endless worldwide assemblies of hearts and minds.

We will attempt to probe this phenomenon presently. But now at the beginning of our ending discussion, let's look beyond entertainment to reality. Let's recall two of the greatest audience responses in world history.

One was the magic elation that swept Paris and the world in the final hours of Charles Lindbergh's transatlantic flight. And greatest of all, by far, was the emotion of millions all over the world watching on television as the first human beings climbed out of Apollo 11 and set foot on the moon.

Those were actual triumphs, of course, transcending the mythology of drama. But each evoked a climax of irrepressible emotion that the filmmaker is always seeking.

People of intelligence and sophistication—to say nothing of pedants and cynics—may minimize audience response to the affirmative ending. Writers dare not.

But they dare not depend on it either. They need only look back at the infancy years of the movies. The banality scoffed at most was the happy ending. Writers wrote subtitles such as: "And so the brave man and the loyal woman rode off into the sunset." The good guys always lived happily ever after. The villain was always shot down in flames.

That constant tie-off in candy-box ribbon was ridiculed because it seemed cheap and unreal. To many a substantial drama it gave the texture of a child's fairy tale. By mindless repetition, the contrived happy ending became ludicrous.

Modern audiences still seek constructive affirmatives (*All the President's Men*). They welcome fantasy trips with fantasy fulfillments (*Star Wars*). But the plastic contrivances of the old happy endings they no longer take seriously.

Sensitive filmmakers of those early years didn't like them much either. Forced to the catchpenny finish by certain bosses, they fumed privately. The infancy years passed; they gained independence—and rebelled.

A countermarch started into the darker country of the downbeat ending. Before long, films were fading out with the hero in a concentration camp, and the girl riding into the sunset of a complete nervous breakdown.

Television was skeptical of bitter negatives, but even their masterpiece line sometimes included a depression special. One of them went something like this:

Coal miners are out of work in a mountain village. To support their starving families they steal coal from the shut-down mines and sell it illegally along the highway.

A social worker discovers that one of the miner's sons has a talent for pottery design, and that the local creek bed produces a rare and marvelous clay. He arranges for the boy to go to the city, learn the ceramics trade, and return to manage a small factory that will be the town's salvation. To finance his trip, starving families dig into socks and teapots for their last pennies.

But the boy discovers that his sweetheart is pregnant, and there are not enough pennies for two, let alone three. If he leaves her behind—even after a last-minute marriage—she will be considered disgraced in the ignorant village.

Conscience compels him to stay home and marry the girl. He and his father sneak back into the mines to steal coal. A cave-in buries both of them alive. His bride is left a lonely widow, to raise a fatherless child. The village is back where it started, facing starvation. Fade out. The bitter end.

The trade has a name for such dark extravagances. They are called *loser stories*. They alienate many audiences because they seem as slanted and unreal as the happy ending.

About now I often see puzzled faces in the classroom. Indignant hands start waving. Am I ruling out tragedy and the tragic ending?

Indeed *not!*

Great tragic tales have always been drama's most enduring staple. They include historical epics, such as the stories of Abraham Lincoln, Christ, Joan of Arc. Also much of Shakespeare. Modern film audiences have acclaimed *A Man for All Seasons*, *Dr. Jekyll and Mr. Hyde*, *Cyrano de Bergerac*, *A Streetcar Named Desire*, *Death of a Salesman*, *King Kong*.

What is the difference, then, between great tragedy and those despairing loser stories?

Very simply, enduring tragic drama usually exalts the human spirit. It offers inspiration, examples of human experience to which all men may aspire. Sometimes tragedy teaches the timeless lesson of man's inhumanity to man. Often it posts a stern warning against self-devotion, as in the legend of Faust. It extols faith, vision, courage that rise above fate and adversity. Its essence is disturbing and magnificent. Enduring tragedy dares man to exceed himself.

On the contrary, the "hero" in many a loser story is a well-meaning misfit who is decimated by life. We find him often the victim of greed, malevolence, hypocrisy. Or of Fate. No matter how hard he tries, he is beaten down and destroyed. He usually dies forlornly, or goes bananas.

Such futile personalities exist in life. Most of us have known heartbreaking examples. Certainly it is every filmmaker's privilege to create such a character story. Some that have been produced have been called masterpieces (the film from Nathanael West's novel *Day of the Locust* was one). But as a practical point in this workbook on screenwriting, you should know that they are among the low percentage shots. Most audiences reject a romantic fascination with defeat. Most "loser" stories are box-office losers. For writers, accordingly, they can be very hard to sell.

Consider a primitive reason for strong audience response to inspiring tragedy, and to rejection of most loser stories.

History is the record of the survival of living organisms over the hostile environment. Since the first amphibians crawled out of the oceans, untold billions have died; but they spawned new species, culminating in man. With his deepest instincts, each man responds to these triumphs of survival against the ultimate enemy.

Today we may be facing the direst tragedy of all—the final war, fought with nuclear power. But even if that horror should happen, the ultimate drama will not be the imbecility of destruction. It will seek out the survivors. It will record their climb back out of sea caves toward life. Heroes will die in that climb. But the classic drama of renewal will immortalize their courage, as they pioneer the saga of mankind anew.

So much for enduring tragedy. And so much for the doubtful extremes—candy-box lovers living happily ever after, and losers that die in despair.

There are other choices—such as "The Lady or the Tiger" ending. This takes its title from an old short story by Frank Stockton.

The heroine, a princess, falls in love with a commoner. Her indignant father, the King, condemns her homespun lover to a cruel choice. Made prisoner, he is placed before two identical doors in the local coliseum. Behind one door is a hungry tiger; behind the other a funky lady in a wedding gown—not the Princess. The prisoner is ordered to open one of the doors, and accept his fate.

But the Princess had done her homework. She knows which door conceals the lady, and which the tiger. From the royal box she flashes a signal to her hero.

There the story ends.

Did the Princess send her lover to his death, or to the arms of the funky bride?

This ingenious take-your-choice ending is a literary trick that rarely succeeds in big-screen drama. As we have found, audiences are like children. No one ever heard a five-year-old say: "Mommy, tell me a story, but don't insult my intelligence by explaining how it comes out."

Kids and audiences are accustomed to dramatic conclusions, like seeing Sleeping Beauty wakened by the kiss of the Prince—or get hacked to death by him (Diane Keaton in *Looking for Mr. Goodbar*). Modern psychology warns us gravely that most people dislike an incomplete or broken pattern. For years football coaches have been grumbling that a tie is like kissing your sister.

The Bittersweet Ending

There remains a final technique for ending your dramatic story. It combines both affirmation and tragedy in the same closing sequence. Fulfillment for some is balanced by sacrifice and often death for others. Stripped down, this usually means that the good guys both win and lose. This most responsive of all third acts has been called the *bittersweet ending*.

Casablanca is a notable example. Humphrey Bogart, you'll remember, is bewitched by Ingrid Bergman. And ditto she by him. Their love lights up the night of Northern Africa. But Bergman has a husband. He is the gentle martyr type, an underground fighter against the Nazis. He depends on Bergman; if she abandons him for Bogart, all his work for the masses will go down the drain. He is wanted by the law. A crowded plane is leaving Casablanca, and Bogart has two flight permits. He gives them to the husband. Love's loss is humanity's gain.

Midnight Cowboy, the Academy's Best Picture of 1969, is another vivid sample Jon Voight, the cowboy, comes to New York to make a career out of sleeping with rich society women.

He fails awkwardly, but he meets a grubby character, played by Dustin Hoffman. Friendship and fierce loyalty develop between them. Hoffman has TB, but believes he could be cured by a trip to Florida. Voight risks prison to steal money for their bus fare. Hoffman dies as they reach Miami. Voight returns to his natural habitat. He has lost the only true friend he ever had, but through their friendship he has discovered human decency.

Memorable versions of the bittersweet ending are legion in fiction and major film. One of the great closing sequences of all romantic storytelling is Sydney Carton's ride to the guillotine in Dickens's *A Tale of Two Cities*. Among America's standout examples are Steinbeck's *Of Mice and Men* (novel, play, film, TV special), and the television masterpiece *My Sweet Charlie*. Chayefsky's Academy Awards for the 1971 and 1976 Best Original Screenplays were won for *The Hospital* and *Network*. Both had bittersweet endings.

Summing Up

If you hope to sell multimillions of tickets to a serious drama, avoid the gooey happily-ever-after finish, as well as the fade-out in total despair.

The first is a relic of a romantic time. Modern audiences have discovered that life never checks out quite that way. The second is equally unreal in the common experience. The human animal has an instinct to survive, and a license to hope, or none of us would be here for next Christmas dinner.

Many great third acts blend the two. The technique often combines a tragic sacrifice with a fulfillment. An honored leader gives his life—so that his disciples may continue the long journey.

Audiences respond to the bittersweet ending because it neither enshrines fantasy nor denies hope.

8.

WHAT AM I GOING TO WRITE ABOUT NEXT?

Story Ideas. Basic Plots. There Is No Such Thing as an Original Story.

Ecstasy for a film or TV writer is typing two magic words on the last page of a script: "THE END."

Pure panic is what follows a couple of days later. "Where can I get another idea? Dear God, what am I going to write about next?"

It may lower the fever if you don't try too hard to find an original story. Because you can't. There is no such thing.

A teacher of the short story at a midwestern university had a standing offer of twenty-five dollars to any student who could turn in a truly virgin plot. No one ever picked the professor's pocket. His computer memory always came up with an earlier essence of the "original" story.

It is widely believed that there are only thirty-six basic dramatic situations. At least a man named George Polti wrote a book to prove it. Some people find his work interminably difficult reading. But scholars have quoted it as gospel.

These basic plots have served imaginative men and women since storytelling started. The specific number hardly matters. Fundamental story lines can be interwoven endlessly to make "new" plots and dramas. What concerns us is that they are every writer's permanent possessions. To illustrate, we will summarize a few enduring samples.

The Faust Story

This story may be the simplest of all, yet so fundamental that it will serve any protagonist in any time. Faust mortgaged his soul to the Devil, raised heaven and hell on the proceeds, and paid off at last with his life.

Mythology, the Bible, and the modern drug scene are full of Fausts. On the big screen we have seen him (and her) self-destruct in *Bonnie and Clyde*, *Taxi Driver*, *Macbeth*, to say nothing of a true-life plot, stranger than any fiction, called Watergate.

The Tragic Flaw, or Character-Change Story

Your protagonist is plagued by a character defect, often called the tragic flaw. The plot forces him to recognize and face his imperfection. At the climax, he (usually) expiates his flaw, or dies trying.

The primordial version is the simple coward story, told around campfires in the Stone Age. As a youth, the protagonist has panicked in battle and run away. Through years of exiled wandering, he comes to terms with his tragic flaw. He returns, at last, with reborn courage, to rescue his village from the enemy.

The tragic flaw can be any human imperfection—self-indulgence, machismo, possessiveness, devil worship, self-deception, insecurity, and dozens more. Among the award and money winners which have told this story are *The Hospital*, *In* the Heat of the Night, Othello, The King and I, Marty, and Midnight Cowboy.

The Eternal Love Story

This is the supreme soap opera, and may be the oldest plot of all. Men and women since life began have been playing out their personal variations.

Boy and girl fall joyously in love. Along the path of heart's desire, they meet fearful obstacles. They either crash through the obstacles and live happily ever after or they die in the end for their love.

Just about every dramatist living, and yet unborn, must write his or her variation. Certified copies will include *As You Like It, Romeo and Juliet, Seventh Heaven, It Happened One Night, My Fair Lady, Guess Who's Coming to Dinner?,* and *Love Story.* You can also write a third act where the lovers don't make it, and your models could be *Gone with the Wind* and *Casablanca.*

Greed Which Destroys

This protagonist, often leading a mixed group, seeks the limitless riches of a secret gold mine, or buried treasure. Finding it, individuals are infected by greed. They start killing each other off to gain sole possession. Usually most of them die in the process, and the treasure is lost.

The classic and constantly copied version is *The Treasure of the Sierra Madre.* But the "original" story has been traced back over two thousand years to Hindu mythology.

A variation remains to be written in which the board of the Writers Guild sends a blue-ribbon committee of distinguished writers on a secret mission. They are to find and bring back to the membership a fabled computer, which contains *all* possible story ideas, characters, plots, and one-liners.

They find it . . .

They are not back yet.

Predestined Tragedy

Usually this is a two-character drama. One of them is doomed to die—perhaps from a terminal illness. Perhaps, if it is the man, he faces a life sentence or the death chair. In many dramatizations, the two fall in love. The story traces their emotional concentrations, as the truth is revealed and the end draws near. An early landmark film was *Dark Victory*, starring Bette Davis. In television, most of the anthologies and all the doctor series have had their versions.

The Damon and Pythias Story

This is the tale of friendship stronger than death. Dionysius, tyrant of Syracuse, condemned Pythias to die. Damon, his inseparable friend, offered to act as his hostage while Pythias went home to settle family concerns. When Pythias missed his return deadline, Damon was marched out to the chopping block. But Pythias checked in just in time to stay the executioner's blade. Their selfless loyalty touched even the tyrant heart of Dionysius, who pardoned both.

This legend goes back to the fourth century B.C. More recent recitals include Dustin Hoffman and Jon Voight in *Midnight Cowboy**, and Jane Fonda and Vanessa Redgrave in the striking distaff version, *Julia*. Both won Academy nominations or awards.

Taste of Honey Formula

This is a modern selection. It is a distinctive example of an identical basic situation played three ways, without imputa-

---

Midnight Cowboy is also listed among the tragic-flaw examples. Duplication is intentional—to show how two (sometimes more) basic situations can be interwoven in a single story.

tion or plagiarism. I wish the great computer were here to tell us its source tale or legend.

In *A Taste of Honey* a pregnant girl is cast out by her family because she has no marriage certificate. Exiled and alone, she is befriended by a male homosexual. Pinch-hitting for both her family and the child's father, he stands by until her baby is born.

Next came the *Kotch* version. Same girl. Pregnant. Outcast. But this time the male character is also adrift in a heartless world. His crime is growing old; his married children have given him the gong because he babbles too much and bores them. Walter Matthau played the part, and movingly. He not only stood by the girl through her pregnancy, but he finagled the baby's father into marrying her.

Finally, the *My Sweet Charlie* version. The pregnant, friendless girl hides out in a coastal summer resort, emptied by winter's cold. A black man appears, fleeing a murder charge. The girl expects rape, inspires compassion. In the climax, the black dies to get her to the hospital in time for her baby's birth. This version became one of the all-time great films made for television.

Thus we have seven basic story structures—all in public domain. Anyone can retell any one of them at any time. And these few are only the beginning.

Any film buff can quote you dozens more. To run down some examples:

The natural disaster drama, so popular in the Seventies— *Earthquake* and *The Poseidon Adventure.*

The Magnificent Seven formula. This served *The Guns of Navarone* and the popular TV series, "Mission: Impossible."

The "Join 'Em to Lick 'Em" plot—the standby of undercover and secret agent tales, as in *The Spy Who Came in from the Cold.*

A recent favorite has been the modern "woman without a husband" dilemma in our society. *The Goodbye Girl* played it for comedy; *Looking for Mr. Goodbar*, for sensation and tragedy; *An Unmarried Woman*, for a slice-of-life social drama. This story, of course, is as old as mating. Its "originality" lies in its equation with changing sex perspectives.

Our basic story concept comes down to this. There are only so many torments that we can inflict on each other, and so many delights we can share. Add the marvels and shocks of fate. Stir them all up together, and you have the sum total of stories that writers can tell.

Where, then, does originality lie?

It lies in your special selection of events and unique treatment of human beings. You are not looking for a wholly new plot structure but for a fresh mixture and interpretation of mortal experiences. Any time, any person, any poison, any triumph are obediently yours. Your originality depends less on where they came from than on where you go with them.

Compare the creative dramatic process with that of any couple producing their dream child. In physical and psychic characteristics, their baby resembles a billion other babies. But we were all babies once. We know that there is no one else remotely like us. We are all master originals.

Expressed as a visual concept, imagine the originalities of three portraits. Subject: the farmer's daughter. Painted from the same model by Michelangelo, Picasso, and Grandma Moses.

Your Starting Point, or Handle

You still need a flash, that specific idea to get you started. Commercially, your best chance is surely a *handle* or *hook* idea. This has also been called, inelegantly, the *grabber*. If it grabs you, it will grab a producer, it will grab an audience. Spectacular samples of this handle follow.

The Exorcist. (Devil possesses young, innocent girl.)

Jaws. (Sharks will eat you if you swim in the ocean.)

Network. (Famed news commentator threatens to kill himself on national television.)

King Kong. (Gigantic ape brought back alive.)
A Case of Rape. (My God, it could happen to me!)

The supply of instant hook notions is obviously limited. But the writer who hopes to sell first a producer, and finally millions of tickets, will do well to consider the principle. Because modern movies cost serious money. Budgets of six, eight, ten, or even twelve million dollars are not uncommon. Thus, properties that most agents and producers look for first are projects with exploitation maximums.

When a writer tells his agent he's got a great new story, the agent's immediate query is, "What's it about?" When the agent brings the manuscript to the producer's desk, that's the latter's first question, "What's it about?"

This question is asked a thousand times a year in Hollywood. When you're looking for commercial action, you had best have a neat answer. Concentrate your story in a short sentence that catches prompt, positive interest.

Really sensational handle ideas, like "Hitler rises from the dead in Pacoima," are in short supply. Beyond that, your top choice is often a character hook.

That is to say, a personality who is immediately appealing, scary, passionate, or otherwise special and interesting. Remember: "Drama favors the great saint or the great sinner." Avoid, therefore, writing about a woman down the street who collects stamps and is pretty boring. Choose, rather, a woman who steals surfboards and is part hyena.

Memorable films with sharp character hooks are legion. For example:

The Hospital, Paddy Chayefsky's award winner about a great doctor who has lost faith in himself as a healer.

Play It Again, Sam, a bumbling Don Juan dreams that he is Humphrey Bogart.

The Godfather and *The Godfather Part II*. Both were violence and crime stories, to be sure. But the dramatic backbone of both was the character study of the *capo.*

Louis Malle, a leading French director, making his debut

in American production, chose *Pretty Baby* by Polly Platt. It was the personality portrait of a girl child born and brought up in a New Orleans whorehouse.

A Social Handle

Your answer to "What's it about?" can be a social indictment. TV's immensely successful *A Case of Rape* was about cruel social and police attitudes toward women they are supposed to protect—rape victims. *Guess Who's Coming to Dinner?* and *In the Heat of the Night* were about racial bigotry. Most war stories nowadays are antiwar stories. Television's *The Glass House* was a brilliant exposé by Truman Capote of inhuman prison conditions. Nothing is more salable than "an idea whose time has come."

The Oldest Obsession

There is nothing wrong about starting with the oldest story in the world, if you gussy it up with fresh, provocative angles. "Boy meets girl," of course, is that oldest story. Remember these striking variations:

A Patch of Blue. A blind girl falls in love with a black man. A variation of that variation was *Butterflies Are Free*, in which a blind boy takes the count for a floozy.

Annie Hall, which won four Oscars, was a "you can't win" romance, a love story of the absurd.

The Eternal Commonplace

About now, I suspect, hackles of protest are rising. What about various successful films that do not have sensational characters or subject matter? Stories about average people, like that Miss Smith we all know who married a Mr. Jones. We have all seen many dramas about less than spectacular characters set against routine backgrounds. How about landmark films like *Sounder*, *Marty*, and *The Last Picture Show*?

You can sell that kind of script if it is superbly written. Brilliant authors have been endowing prosaic characters with audience appeal since the story trade started. A truly gifted dramatist can create an absorbing play about the invention of tapioca pudding.

But that is surely the hard way. If you respect statistics and want to play the percentages, consult the Academy Awards lists. You'll find the majority of winners deal with special people confronting unique or unusual situations.

Thus, your starting point or handle may be a character you've discovered, a strange incident, an injustice that makes you mad. It may be a miracle in some friend's marriage; an unexpected twist or solution that can work as your third act. It may be a horror, or a haunting salvation.

Source Materials

Where, then, do those special situations, and those unique people come from?

From everywhere. Ideas bombard us from all directions in these days of sandblast communications. Air and print news, books old and new, periodicals, cartoons, history, crime and punishment, movies, hundreds of TV programs daily. All of them abound with ideas and people. In fact, our eyes, ears, and brains tend to become complacent, careless. Even numb.

This suggests that a story maker's urgent priority should be *awareness*. A writer is always in his working clothes. An example from years ago comes back to me.

An unheralded screenwriter was driving his two daughters home from school one California afternoon. They saw two young soldiers hitchhiking and gave them a lift. The girls were in their young teens, and to enhance their image they began telling tall tales of sophistication.

Papa, in the front seat, couldn't hear them because of

traffic noises. But he had to stop for a traffic signal. Waiting for the light to turn green, he heard the girls feeding the soldiers some hype about a high-school girl friend who had actually become pregnant! Remember, this was in the simplistic long ago, when academic pregnancy was an unmentionable catastrophe.

Our screenwriter dramatized that flight of fancy into a stage comedy called *Kiss and Tell*. A smash hit on Broadway, it sold expensively to Hollywood. It ran for years as a radio serial, and became a successful TV series.

That author's name was F. Hugh Herbert. He wrote other rewarding plays, notably *The Moon Is Blue*, and many outstanding films. He became president of the Writers Guild. He parlayed those few seconds of awareness at a traffic light into both fame and fortune.

Such awareness begins with the live action around you. Newspapers and newscasts are full of it. They do not thrive on their editorials; they sell dramatic stories about what's happening, and the freaks and the famous that it's happening to.

Factual reading—history, biography, memoirs—can be especially rewarding. Even tales of characters and times long past. Cultures change, but people keep right on doing the same damn things. A baroque old chronicle can give you a protagonist, a point of view, a human paradox.

But handle truth—ancient or modern—with care. I often get plot outlines with the notation, "This really happened to my drunken uncle." That doesn't make it deathless drama. "Facts," someone has said, "are an inferior form of fiction." You, the dramatist, must distill the substance, and you must communicate the meaning.

Your final area of special awareness should be radio, films, and television. Carl Reiner, the brilliant writer-director-producer-actor who typifies the professional's professional, was asked on a TV talk show for his best advice to an aspiring writer.

"Watch all the movies and TV that you can," he said. "Not to copy them, but so you will *know the clichés*."

Schools and colleges across America are introducing more and more studies in film and television. Talking to students and faculty on various wanderings, I have encountered a strange snobbishness. Many students can't be bothered watching weekly TV; they won't waste their time on anything but outstanding feature films.

The routine junk bores them. Damn right it does. No magic will ever be found 'to fill those ravenous hours with brilliance and inspiration.

Those students are going to classes to learn some creative techniques. My best advice to them is that one really bad picture is worth ten pages of good advice. When you have been disappointed, bored, or maybe hit in the gut by a garbage can, then you are less likely to make those mistakes yourself.

One of the brightest students I was ever fortunate enough to have in my class spent the whole course preparing an idea for a new TV series. He worked it out in detail, including a full pilot script. He wouldn't discuss it in class, and he didn't even submit it to me for comment until the final week. Then he swore me to darkest secrecy. His series hero was a salesman from the Colt Arms Company in New England. He was sent west as an expert with their new .45-caliber hand gun. In each episode, he sold his merchandise by a super exhibition of killing the bad guy.

TV wallowed in westerns in those days, and the constant search was for a new type of righteous gunslinger. So this was a pretty good idea. So good, in fact, that it was already being broadcast that season as a popular weekly series called "Colt .45." My prize student hadn't stolen the idea. He had just goofed on his awareness. He hadn't bothered to watch any routine television.

Some Guidelines for Story Selection

A Modern Story. If you ask twenty agents what type of material they would prefer to sell, and twenty producers what they would prefer to buy, most of them will tell you "a modern story."

Strangely enough, box-office records do not bear out this preference. Of the dozen or fifteen top grossers worldwide, more than half played out in past or future settings. These include *Gone with the Wind*, *The Godfather*, *The Sound of Music*, *The Sting*, *Doctor Zhivago*, *Butch Cassidy and the Sundance Kid*, and *Star Wars*.

Despite such statistics, writers cannot disregard this prejudice in favor of contemporary material. Most story buyers believe that present-day youth audiences prefer present-day plots. Beyond that, modern stories are a lot less trouble to produce, and a lot cheaper, than movies about men in square-rigged ships fighting over square-rigged women.

A Youth Story. The second species that producers often favor is the "youth" story. Again, they warrant that a predominantly thirty-or-under audience prefers stories about younger people. And again, this is hard to justify. *Grease*, *American Graffiti*, and *Saturday Night Fever* are the only effectively "youthful" scripts among recent top grossers. Moreover, few major "youth" stars (like John Travolta) are available during a given season. The fact is that most worldwide box-office hits are built around men and women in their thirties, forties, or even fifties.

But that's pushing the age limit—unless you're Henry Fonda or Katharine Hepburn. Be advised that films about older people and their special problems are hard to sell because they post spotty box-office records. Even brilliant films like Victor Moore and Beulah Bondi's long-forgotten *Make Way for Tomorrow*, Gene Hackman and Melvyn Douglas in *I Never Sang for My Father*, and Art Carney in *Harry and Tonto* were not among the top hits of their seasons.

Constructive Endings. If you isolate any single component that earns consistent audience favor, it would have to be constructive or affirmative stories. This does not—repeat not—

mean old-fashioned syrupy, "happy endings." It means films that tackle social or personal problems and suggest solutions, themes that post warnings or offer inspiration, concepts with positive moral and emotional substance. Stories such as *Julia* and *All the President's Men*.

This whole matter is so complex and so essential that we have devoted a large part of an earlier chapter to it (see Chapter 7, "Ending a Dramatic Story"). Again, we suggest a reexamination.

Sex and Violence. Only a fool or a hypocrite would ignore the box-office harvest of sex and violence. Certainly a great many producers are looking for stories that legitimately exploit these two elements. How any writer or producer defines "legitimately " of course, is his own personal business.

Crime and Punishment Stories. Violence floods into crime, detective, and police shows. It disfigures some of them by its excess; its skillful use adds frightening impact to others.

Stories of violent crime and gory punishment go back forever. The old gods themselves were often violent despots. The Greeks and Romans spun "pursuit of evil" tales around three goddesses called the Furies. Those three girls—on behalf of crime victims, their friends and families—pursued and punished killers and evildoers. The Furies were the great, great, great grandmothers of Sherlock Holmes, Sam Spade, and Angie Dickinson. Public response to them is immemorial. Creative stories about crime and punishment will always be in demand.

The Woman's Story. Amid the current welter of crime, sex, and violence films, a totally different type of story has surfaced. That is the so-called *woman's story*.

Films like *The Turning Point*, *Julia*, and *An Unmarried Woman* attract box-office lines to theaters all over the world. To be sure, there have always been women's classics, like *Rain*, *Camille*, and *A Doll's House*. But for years, male stars and male stories have dominated a medium that thrives on visual action. Maybe male chauvinism had something to do with it. In any case, profit figures on women's stories suggest that they have come to stay.

While sales chances for women's stories are climbing sharply, let's still be practical. Beware of flagrant soap opera — stories about routine female domestic or romantic problems. To be sure, every now and then material like *Peyton Place* or *Love Story* comes along and makes a big hit. And this does *not* mean that you should not try love stories. Great love dramas are staples of the craft. But soap opera is a love story in Dullsville. Myrtle learns that her massive boy friend from Alaska is secretly married to an Eskimo. Or woman stuck with boring husband meets charming architect. But he smokes opium and raises skunks. What shall she do? In other words, peculiarly feminine dilemmas that make great gossip sessions—but won't fascinate audiences which include lots of males and modern young people.

A woman's story should be *about something*—as well as about women.

Westerns. As women's stories gain front-office favor, we find a great American male figure crashing down. That is the classic western lawman. An agent told me recently that the whole western concept is a forgotten fantasy, impossible to present seriously to a modern producer.

This indignity will last, of course, only until a big new smash hit western comes along. Decision makers in show business are like chickens. Throw out a scoop of corn, and they all rush to the same place. Westerns have been staples of our craft and of our culture. *The Virginian*, written in 1902 by Owen Wister, started a legend which was sustained by *The Covered Wagon* (the first million-dollar movie), *Cimarron*, *Stagecoach*, *High Noon*, *True Grit*, and hundreds more. "Gunsmoke" was the longest-running series in the history of television.

Westerns are not only hot dog and apple pie America. They have a steadfast worldwide audience. Fan clubs called

Corrals dot this country and have sprung up in European and Oriental cities. A respected French critic said that America has made only two original contributions to the arts. Those two: jazz and the western.

Science Fiction. That endangered species—the western—has been replaced in the hearts of the new generation by science fiction. Today's heroes shoot lasers instead of six-guns, and ride spaceships in place of horses. Sensational profits from *Star Wars* and *Close Encounters of the Third Kind* will keep their futuristic fires burning, perhaps for years. In fact some sages are predicting that science fiction may become a routine story staple, like police shows or family stories. Only time, and perchance some box-office disaster from outer space, will tell. Certainly, mature science fiction offers the ultimate in challenges to creative imagination.

Action-Adventure. Both westerns and science fiction are modern offspring of the oldest and bestselling story of all. That is the action-adventure tale.

The same agent who recently condemned westerns told me—almost in the same breath—"Give me a strong action-adventure story, and I can sell it anywhere."

Action-adventure is not just a sugar substitute term for violence. Many action-adventure movies involve violence, but the great ones are stories of human character. Examples: *The African Queen*, *The Bridge on the River Kwai*, *Mutiny on the Bounty*, *Lawrence of Arabia*, *King Kong*, *Treasure Island*, and *Superman*. All war stories are action-adventure; all sea stories. The visual sweep of such material was made for movies. It has eternal dramatic and sales appeal.

The Essential Ingredient

For your final, gut ingredient in choosing story material, you do well to look beyond percentages and Neilsen ratings.

Do you care about those people in your story? Do you

believe in them? Do you mean those burning words that you have given them to say?

In the writing trade, you are committed to audience communication. That audience out front is as necessary to your show as you are. You convey meaning to those listening millions through feeling.

They should tremble before your heavy. Every woman should be in bed with your hero, and every man with that enchanting girl.

Remember what Frank Capra said: "The whole thing is—you've got to make them *care* about somebody."

If you do—they will.

9.

DIALOGUE

"The Secret of Being a Crushing Bore Is to Say Everything."

David O. Selznick hired many of the leading writers of America in his years as the top independent producer of the industry. He once told me that he regarded Zoë Akins as about the best dialogue writer in the business.

Zoë Akins was a Pulitzer Prize–winning playwright who came out of the Broadway theater to write major movies Selznick's admiration for her dialogue was not due to her memorable epigrams or prismatic style. Her scenes didn't jump off the page at you. "They just sounded like people talking," said Selznick. "And they played!"

There is only one way to make actors reading dialogue sound like people talking. That is by listening. That factor is so fundamental that I've saved a detailed discussion of it for the end of the chapter. But before we start exploring techniques, let's examine aspects of film and TV writing generally.

Much of the dialogue you hear in big-screen movie houses

these days is soundly professional. Often it is absolutely excellent. For two good reasons.

Topflight film authors are the highest paid writers since people started putting words on paper. Their salary levels in most cases reflect their competence. Furthermore, they can pick projects that appeal to them, and demand enough time to do each job justice. Finally, producers of high-budget films, directors, and major actors have studied those pages vigilantly. Every word is rehearsed before the camera turns.* Clichés and tongue-twisters have gone out with the trash.

By contrast, scripts for TV episodic series are often written at high speed. Ceiling pay for a one-hour dramatic episode is around $8,000. During high activity months, hot writers often work on more than one project at a time. Producers are chronically in a rush for those vital pages.

It is true that uniquely capable people (Sterling Silliphant, for example, when he used to toil in TV) can produce fifty or sixty pages a week without compromising quality. But most writers, to turn out their best work, have to write and rewrite, revise the rewrite, and then sometimes tear that up and start all over. That is classic and chronic in most fields of writing. Words are relentless. You just have to sit there and sweat over them.

For your best dialogue, you dig a little deeper inside you. Those words on the surface are mostly carbon copy talk. Check your own casual conversation and that of friends. Only occasionally do they—or you—ad-lib a sentence worth carving in stone. Yet characters in good scripts must speak provocative

---

* Movie producers vary wildly, and so do their preparation procedures. Certain writer-directors like John Cassavetes encourage actors to improvise dialogue scenes on the set. Robert Blake claims that much of the often skillful chatter in his "Baretta" series is spontaneous. There have always been such individualists, but they are a volatile minority. Most producers, directors, and stars prefer to have word patterns tested before the day's filming starts.

lines as a matter of course. A film or TV play (even a cop show or western) should deal in wisdom and humor and punch lines.

We have found that originality in story material is strictly limited. The theme, the basic human emotions of your script— you *must* repeat. But your characters must still seem fresh and original. Your main chance to make them seem so lies in giving them fresh and original things to say. Plus new ways of saying them.

But—let me quickly warn you—don't try *so* hard that the words are different—but phony. Nothing is so awful as forced, high-flown, purple talk. Example: a western years ago starring some pokey old trapper like Chill Wills. At the very end he got philosophical, this old western primitive, and he used the word *incandescence.* That one word burned down the whole characterization.

In Defense of Writers
Indignities and Mutilations Department

No matter what speeches are typed in your final TV script, sometimes actors, directors, or producers rewrite them. I remember the closing day on the set of a show a student of mine had written. He had asked me over to watch them shoot the moving climax. The star of the series swept in with a hangover (names are omitted to protect the guilty). He launched into the key speech, and his thick tongue blew it. He tried it again, blew it higher. He got mad, started blaming the writer, wasting time.

Delay the director could not afford. Hour-long television shows are shot on a tight one-week schedule. He calmed the actor down by telling him to forget the script and just say it his way. He did, and the result was disastrous. Panic rewrites on the set, like this, come from the top layer, where the hoariest clichés live.

The writer has no recourse, no protection in contracts. A producing company buys the legal right to change anything the author has written. But the writer gets the public blame, since his name is up there in the screen credits. Even a sympathetic producer can't cut a subtitle into his film saying that his star had a hangover.

Fairness cries out that we flip this coin over and look at the brighter side. Conscientious directors and actors work their tails off to make slapdash dialogue sound alive and special. Beyond that are those rare moments when truly challenging lines are read by a gifted actor or actress. Such readings can add beauty and meaning even the author never realized. When that magic mix happens to you, it is one of the bright satisfactions of the screenwriting craft.

Conflict

Selznick's second essential of good dialogue was that the scene *played.* The classic, all but infallible, device to achieve this is to write that scene in conflict.

Words are weapons. They can be blunt instruments, or rapier sharp. Characters in verbal conflict are the mainspring of dramatic or comedic writing.

Chapter 3 of this book is devoted to conflict. Nowhere in the dramatic process is conflict more necessary than in dialogue. But since repetition is a special sin, we won't rehash those pages. Instead, why not cut in a flashback?

Love Scenes

A love scene is the primeval cliché. Adam whispered the same adoring words to Eve that all the Antonys ever since have said to all the Cleopatras. Several minutes of this honeydew can get faintly nauseating. Why do you think directors get their lovers into bed so fast these days?

J. Walter Ruben, a producer-director with whom I worked on many scripts at MGM, had a flat rule. The words, "I love you," could never be heard in any film of his. Because, simply and truly, it is the oldest cliché in our language. Beyond that, he said, it has been spoken on stage so many thousands of times that no actor alive could give it a fresh reading.

Poets, it is true, can set clichés to divine music. But be sure you are at least a minor poet before you try. Beyond that, the two escape hatches for love scenes are conflict and comedy.

In *The Goodbye Girl* Neil Simon fashioned almost an entire script out of conflict-comedy love scenes. Recall the opening scenes of *Love Story* (a soaring success whether everybody liked it or not)—Ali MacGraw was insulting Ryan O'Neal, and they were falling furiously in love. Those were standard love scenes in conflict. They *played!*

Of course, *Gone with the Wind* is the classic conflict love story of them all. Jump cut forty years from that to almost any love passage between Diane Keaton and Woody Allen. Theirs are usually love scenes on the wry side. But millions of people, including many who vote distinguished achievement awards, love them dearly. Anytime you can keep audiences laughing, they will swallow a lot of toasted marshmallows.

Period Pieces and Dialects

Period is an inexact term in a youth culture that regards the 1930s as the Middle Ages. But when the film trade speaks of a period piece, it signifies a drama in which the clothes, architecture, and manners of speech are museum exhibits.

Every historical epoch, each tribe, and each country had specialized speech patterns. If you and I were suddenly switched back to Chaucer's England, we would not understand most of what the people were saying, even though we knew it was English.

Therefore, if you are writing a film about Chaucer, you cannot use Chaucerian English. Your audience simply would not be able to make head or tail of it. So, what do you do?

You fashion it for yourself, in expressive modern English. Then you antique it. If you are conscientious, you dig out some true Chaucerian writing at the library and try to make your English sound remotely like it. Remember, however, that the meanings must be crystal clear to an audience that is only casually literate. Perhaps you substitute archaic words, or invert sentence construction. Take the modern gloss off it with Old World phrasing.

In other words, you make it *sound* like people talking in that earlier culture. As dialogue in the Bible, for example, sounds like tongues wagging in the Holy Land over two thousand years ago. I'm sure that millions of people hearing a Bible story read on the radio or in church assume that is how Moses, Rebecca, or John the Baptist really talked. Yet the cherished Church of England Bible is the King James version. That was written seventeen centuries after Christ, in London, by Englishmen.

With a living, or modern, vernacular you have to be more careful. Think how you squirm when a London film writer tries to write American gang jive. Think how he squirms when you take a wild shot at his Welsh or Cockney. When you're faced with such a problem, try to find some stories, plays, or recordings in the authentic idiom. Read the print aloud to yourself. Listen to the recordings for flavor and cadence. In short, do your homework.

Certain living dialects are even more elusive. Years ago I wrote a Howard Hawks film called *Tiger Shark*, starring Edward G. Robinson. Robinson played a tuna boat captain out of San Diego. His dialect was Portuguese-American, complicated by the tuna fleet jargon. I went down to the San Diego docks and talked to some living originals. Their lingo was so strange, so specialized, that I knew we would never get it right on the set. So the studio hired a real Portuguese tuna captain to edit the script with me, and to stand by Robinson throughout shooting. The three of us worked over every speech. The tuna man's job was to make it authentic, mine to make it comprehensible.

This was a special case, to be sure. But it recommends that you take all the trouble you can to research a dialect background. For two practical reasons.

1. If your jargon is careless and phony, your producer will get abusive letters. He will blame—not illogically—the writer.
2. But if you do take that extra trouble, you will earn a rare dividend. Genuine dialect makes your characters sound original, alive, and true.

Modernisms in Period Dialogue. This is such a flagrant malpractice that it gets a subdivision of its own.

How many times have you seen a western in which the saintly saloon girl tells the heavy, "Drop dead, buster!" No records exist which tell us that "drop dead" or "buster" were not pearls of the pioneer idiom. But we all know them as clichés of twentieth-century slang. If they pop up in period dialogue they shout at you that the writer, director, or producer simply wasn't paying attention. Worse than that, they destroy the scene's mood and illusion.

When a well-born British lady of two hundred years ago calls her titled lover a weirdo, or the pits, then you're not in eighteenth-century London anymore.

Of course, such oversights are chiefly characteristic of action films and slapdash television. Thus they don't deeply concern big screenwriters and directors. The hell they don't! I once heard, "Okay, let's get going," in a stately epic about the Crusades. The bigger the budget, the more unforgivable such carelessness.

Curse of the Cliché

Clichés are the degenerative taint of television dialogue. In one week not so long ago a student of mine caught "Get off my back" in eight different TV episodes. Next to "I love you," the all-tube champion cliché has got to be "Are you all right?" Remember "Groovy," and "Love is never having to say you're sorry"?

TV and film dialogue have another old failing called the *cliché superlative*. It is a characterization device:

"Joe's the toughest guy in the ghetto."

"She's the sexiest girl on the beach."

"He's the richest dude in Encino."

The device is lazy writing for three reasons. It is worn out. It is indefinite. It offers no specific comparison.

There is even a master cliché in writing about writing. That is the instructor's ceaseless warning against clichés. Perhaps we had all better skip this section, because it is so very obvious.

Let's not forget that audiences aren't so lucky. They can't skip. They have to sit there and listen.

The Efficient Blue Pencil

When you're very young and you finish your first screenplay, the words seem to glow with a strange magic—because *you* wrote them. That's good; indulge yourself. I remember how I felt long ago walking around New York with my first manuscript. It seemed so light that I kept putting my hand in my pocket to make sure it was there!

But the next day, come on down to reality. Get to work on those precious scenes, especially the dialogue. There are no brand-new stories. But many things that happen to us, happen for the first time. Life, in that sense, is bright with eternal youth. That's how you should make it sound on paper.

The first aim of your rewrite is to squeeze out the snow. Cut, condense, intensify, tighten.

Dialogue for films and television is a specialized telegraphic language. Make a tape recording of any rap session with your friends. You will find, on replaying it, that you can edit out perhaps a third or more—and still everybody will be saying the same thing.

Screen dialogue seeks only that essence. Furthermore, and strangely so, the very finest line sometimes leaves something to the imagination. It depends on a hidden element called the *subtext.* That is the secret meaning, the extra truth that your audience supplies. A gentle threat that suggests a deadly horror. The "or-else" warning with its hint of havoc and bloody bones.

Be thus keenly aware, as you edit your dialogue, that a hidden subtext your spectator provides may be more dramatic than the words your actors speak. Set the audience's imagination to work for you. As writers, we can all profit from some advice Van Gogh gave to artists: "Paint the gesture, not the hand."

The rewrite process can have a special significance for students and nonprofessional writers. In years of reading workshop scripts, I have found that some beginners are in awe of their dialogue. They tend to be too precise, too complete. They try too hard to cover all the bases. This can result in formal, balanced speeches, answered by ponderous, balanced replies. Real people's dialogue never comes down like that. Your actors will sound like programmed robots giving read-outs.

The remedy, of course, is manifest. Humanize the scene by breaking up those formal speeches. Dare your people to interrupt each other. Let one of them lose his cool; we all get mad, especially when cornered. A flash of sudden wit will vitalize any scene. Most of all, try to make the *feeling*, not just the facts, come through.

The ultimate wisdom about editing dialogue came from Voltaire, one of the French immortals. I suspect that he was speaking not only to writers, but to man- and womankind everywhere. "The secret of being a crushing bore," he warned, "is to say everything."

Speech Structure and Design

Often the design of a significant dialogue speech is like that of a story. Your beginning states the premise, catches the hearer's interest. Your middle intensifies it. Your finish is the punch position, the convincer.

This device of building to the closing phrase of your

speech may be the most practical aid you can absorb about writing dramatic dialogue. Check every significant speech in your script, because you don't necessarily make it on your first draft.

You may find that you have the punch line up front, or in the middle of the speech. Perhaps you have been so pleased with that punch line that you have added a weakening repetition. This dilutes the emphasis. Never try to top your topper.

If you are still in doubt about it, remember the classic construction of a joke. The punch line is *always* the tag. That's what explodes the big laugh. In a dramatic speech you are after an emotional rush that corresponds to that responding laugh.

Examples are classic, not only in literature, but throughout history. No American speech ever had the end punch of Lincoln's "So that government of the people, by the people, for the people shall not perish from the earth."

The humbler areas of dramatic writing for film and television offer endless opportunities. The following example carries just the right emotion for its moment in the script. It comes from *Farewell to Manzanar,* a TV dramatization of California-Japanese interned in prison camps during World War II.

The father of the Japanese family is under interrogation. He was born in Japan but has prospered in America; all his children are American citizens. He is asked harshly by the American officer:

"Who do you want to win the war, the United States or Japan?"

After a moment's thought, he answers, with a Japanese accent. "When your mother and father are fighting, you don't want either of them to kill the other. You just pray that they will stop fighting."

Note how the opening grabs your attentive imagination. The middle builds interest. The last line is the climax, the convincer.

Now read exactly the same words, putting the punch line in the middle. "When your mother and father are fighting, you just pray that they will stop fighting. You don't want either of them to kill the other." Note the deadened dramatic effect.

Give your speeches their best shot. Check their construction design.

Troubleshooting Tip

Now and then every writer gets stuck fast on a difficult line of dialogue. Perhaps you have tried it over and over until it's gotten forced and lumpy. A stubborn line like that can kill you for half a morning.

Don't let it. Throw away all those false starts and ask yourself this question:

"What would he or she *really* say?"

Write the answer down as simply and as clearly as possible, *always shunning the cliché*. Just the direct essence. Your line may not be Shakespearean, but it will ram you through the roadblock. Now you can finish your scene, and keep on going. Probably you will get a new flash tomorrow.

But tomorrow the line may fool you by working just as it is. Simplicity can kick like a mule.

Talking to Yourself

Everybody in today's world is looking for a slave gadget, an artificial helper that will do the work of working. A dialogue writer has two.

Oldest and most reliable are your vocal cords. Dialogue lines are written to be spoken by actors with mikes dangling over their heads. If you want to hear how they sound ahead of time—and you should—read those lines aloud to an audience of one. You have no idea how this will expose rocks and wads of cotton in those precious speeches. Remember that your words are not precious to any actor, unless they come easily to his tongue.

Act that actor. Play all those scenes throughout your

script. Forget what your words look like on paper. Discover how they *sound* when someone has to say them.

Your second slave gadget is a tape recorder. These machines have become so handy and reliable that more and more writers are experimenting with them. Sitting in your car, or on a quiet mountaintop, you can verbalize dialogue straight to your private sound track.

But perhaps even more useful is the recorder's role as dialogue playback. Dictate that dialogue scene you have written, and try it over on yourself as critic. The playback will reveal weak spots; it will lay bare repetitions; it will expose jawbreakers.

And if you doubt you could be guilty of a jawbreaker, hear this one. It was written by a truly distinguished California writer in a star-studded story of the American military. A WAC sergeant comes rigidly to attention and barks out this order:

"All those holding orders for Fort Oglethorpe, fall out!"

Try it aloud.

Conclusions

Bad dialogue is blood kin to flat or off-pitch music. Anyone who insists on writing for films or television should perhaps arrange to be born with a true ear, an instinct for people talking.

There is, however, another view. Paddy Chayefsky said: "As long as what you are saying is true, dialogue isn't all that important. Personally, I think that Eugene O'Neill wrote atrocious dialogue; but nobody will argue his worth as a dramatist."

Whether your ear is divinely tuned or not, don't be too worried. How many times has the following happened?

You are at a bar or a party. Some smart-ass makes a crack, and perhaps you're the target. You struggle for a comeback, and you're tongue-tied. But on your way home, or before you fall asleep that night, you think of the punch line that would have flattened the rat.

That is the dialogue writer's advantage. He has all night, or all week, to dream up the ideal comeback. As head writer of your own scenes you have added privilege. You design the insult as well as the counterpunch.

Never worry if genius eludes you on the first try. Take time, dig deep down in there, and you will almost certainly find that you have more dialogue skill than you supposed.

The Sound of People Talking. Years ago a gifted writer and story editor, James Menzies, spoke one evening to my workshop students at UCLA. About their dialogue, he asked them this question:

"Are you listening?"

He suggested that anyone who wants to write must be tuned in to the live force of words around him. The writer should develop a mental echo chamber that catches the tone and cadence of people talking.

A painter generally works from a model, or perhaps a living landscape. Seldom does he create out of his own head. But a writer has to. So you must listen closely to the sound of people talking, if you want to reproduce it.

Listen to people in your market, on the beach, in buses, on television and talk shows when they have salty, off-beat characters on the program. Listen to street people chattering in "the smeary argot of the slums."

Never trust a great phrase to your memory. Jot it down, or tape-record it. Every so often transfer the best entries to a master list. This will tune your attention to people talking, and add up to a priceless savings account—all free.

A thousand vivid phrases are kicked around the streets for every one that is coined by writers. Creative imagination has been defined as "a new mixture of memories." Start a dialogue memory bank.

Are you listening?

10.

PUTTING YOUR SCRIPT ON PAPER

Style and Format for Movies and Filmed Television

When a film or television writer sits down to put his script on paper, he wears a double hat—sight and sound. For the eye of the camera he describes his visual elements—his people, animals, machines, their surroundings, and what they are doing. For the ear of the microphone he sets down spoken dialogue, gunfire, the first cry of a baby, tires screaming.

His script is not an art form, nor a composition for public sale. It is the work diagram for a manufacturing process. Its primary readers will be his producer, director, cameraman, actors, editorial supervisor, film editor, and the production office.

This may sound complex and technical. It need not be. No good writer was ever kicked out of the promised land for not digging camera angles. What producers, directors, and actors seek from a script are human characters and emotions, laughs, fantasy, conflict, and idea content. They will translate these into practical prismatics on the screen.

But since your script is a blueprint for artists, craftsmen, and cost accountants, you had best follow the seasoned format. Picture people are visual readers. They will know what you mean instantly.

The formats for films and filmed television are, for the most part, identical.* We'll examine the standard format, and reprint an inspired sample of just what it looks like, in a few moments. First let's flash back to earliest silent movie days, and see how this work diagram for dreams started.

When those crude one-reelers were first hand-cranked, this book could not have existed. Because there was no such thing as a screenwriter. Indeed, there were no formal, written screenplays.

Those earliest producer-directors flashed on a one-reel idea, and perhaps jotted down a few notes. Hiring some actors, they extemporized the silent scenes, and started shooting then and there. The only actual writing done was the handful of silent *titles*, written, shot, and cut in later, to clarify the stuttering action.

Very soon they discovered that ideas developed on the set during shooting—gags, laughs, shocks, bits of business. Actors or others with nimble minds went on payroll to stand behind the camera and make suggestions. But still these earliest movie authors were not called writers. They were known as gagmen.

This ad-lib procedure proved wasteful. Too much time was spent brightening up scenes, while leading actors stood around drawing salaries and drinking coffee. So gagmen were hired ahead of time, and housed in an office to hatch their brain children.

Something known as a *scenario*, or *continuity*, developed. It was the story told in a numbered list of camera set-ups,

---

* A somewhat different format is customary for live and videotaped television, and for TV situation comedy. Also, some movie and TV producers are idiosyncratic. A writer familiar with standard format can pick up these variations in minutes.

called scenes. Each scene described the action to be photographed from that camera position. The progressive pattern of these scenes provided a continuity of story line. Occasional printed titles were written, photographed, and cut in, to interpret players' lip movements and to clarify plot development.

Two distinct professions emerged. One was screenwriting. That was the craft of telling a story, silently, in progressive motion-picture patterns. The second is now a totally lost art— silent title writing. Top title writers in the Twenties earned thousands of dollars a week for what was lyrically described as "weaving wall mottoes for the deaf and dumb racket."

Then, with the Thirties, *talkies* inundated the screen. Words and music became the consorts of silent action. Printed titles gave way to spoken dialogue. A script format evolved which combined the action blueprint of the old silent films with the new dialogue and sound elements. That format, basically, is in common use today.

The quickest way to decode this modern format is to take a thoughtful look at it. To this end, we have created a dramatic specimen of what a movie or filmed TV script looks like on paper. Much of it explains itself. The technical jargon yields to question and answer (included). The personal story is utterly without redeeming social value, except as a technological illustration.

TAKE IT FROM THE TOP
FADE IN

1   EXT. STUDIO ENTRANCE—ESTABLISHING SHOT—DAY
A sign over the entrance identifies XYZ STUDIOS. Film
people are thronging through the gate, climbing into
waiting cars, calling "good night" to each other.

2   CLOSER SHOT AT GATE
A GIRL on foot is bucking traffic to enter the studio. At the
entrance kiosk, she receives a pass from the COP, and he
points direction down the studio street. She thanks him
and maneuvers through the crowd.

BEGIN TITLES OVER

3   STUDIO STREET
The girl comes down the studio street, looking around with
the eager curiosity of a visitor. She is a very neat girl,
intelligent, dressed in native funk. This is obviously our
heroine, a character larger than life, including her bosom.

4— ATMOSPHERE SHOTS IN STUDIO
9   A series of picturesque angles on studio sets and people
offer visual b.g. for the CONTINUING TITLES. The girl
dodges ACTORS and ELEPHANTS, their work done,
heading home to the hay. She checks her pass, having
difficulty finding her way. CLOWNS and AMAZONS help
her. She spots a building across the street.

10 DETAIL SHOT FROM GIRL'S POV
A plaque beside the entrance designates:

WRITER'S BUILDING

11 GIRL ON STREET
She ducks across through the thinning traffic, and goes
into the Writer's Building.

END TITLES

12 INT. WRITER'S OFFICE—FULL SHOT
The office is small, modestly furnished with a couch,
CONTINUED

12   CONTINUED
     threadbare rug, and easy chair. At the desk, hunched over
     his typewriter, is the WRITER. He is a stringy old gobbler,
     and a fast hunt-and-peck typist. Hearing a KNOCK at the
     door, he yells.

                    WRITER
          C'mon in!

13   ANGLE FAVORING DOOR
     The girl enters She looks around with wide-eyed curiosity.

                    GIRL
          Hi

                    WRITER (V.O.)
          Hi. Where did you come from?

                    GIRL
          Why ... I come from small towns, big cities,
          ghettos, junior colleges, universities. I come
          from all those seething millions who want
          to break into the movies.

     She moves over to his desk as they talk, CAMERA
     ADJUSTING.

                    WRITER
               (reassuringly)
          Writing's your best chance. Here in
          Hollywood we've got great directors, actors,
          cameramen. Everything but creative
          scripts.

                    GIRL
          And we all have great ideas, marvelous
          characters, but we don't know how to put
          them on paper. I've come for the chapter
          on FORMAT.

                    WRITER
          It's almost finished. I've written an original
          to illustrate it for you.

                                        CONTINUED

13 CONTINUED

He collects pages, and holds them out to her.

> GIRL
> An original story ... But that's fantastic of
> you!
> (takes pages)
> Thanks ...

> WRITER
> Read my opening sentence aloud. Ask me
> questions.

> GIRL
> (starting to read script aloud)
> Fade in ... Ext ... studio entrance ...
> establishing shot ... day.

14 CLOSE SHOT—FIRST PAGE OF SCRIPT
This is a replica of the opening of the script which began
our illustration. The girl's voice continues, reading those
same opening script directions.

> GIRL (V.O.)
> A sign over the entrance identifies XYZ
> Studios. Film people are thronging through
> the gate, climbing into waiting cars, calling
> "good night" to each other.
> (beat)
> Closer shot at gate. A girl on foot is bucking
> traffic to enter the studio.

15 INDIVIDUAL SHOT—GIRL
She breaks off reading, puzzled and provoked.

> GIRL
> I'm confused. That girl outside the studio
> sounds like me. Is this some kind of
> crummy joke?

16   TWO SHOT—GIRL AND WRITER

> **WRITER**
> Dear girl, do I understand that you have
> read the earlier chapters of my book?

> **GIRL**
> I know them by heart.

> **WRITER**
> Then what is the single most important
> element a writer must put in a dramatic
> story?

> **GIRL**
> (carefully)
> Why, empathy with the leading characters
> ... that's Chapter 2 ... you've got to make
> them <u>care</u> about somebody!

> **WRITER**
> So whom does everybody care about most?
> (beat)
> You, for example. Be honest.

> **GIRL**
> (thinking, then)
> Why .. myself, I suppose.

17   CLOSE SHOT—GIRL
She looks back to script.

> **GIRL**
> This girl in your script <u>is me!</u>
> (directly to writer)
> But I am also the reader!
> (beat)
> Why, you sneaky old bastard!

18   BACK TO TWO SHOT

> **WRITER**
> Flattery will not fill your doggie bag. You
> (MORE)

CONTINUED

18   CONTINUED

> WRITER
> want to learn script format? Take it from
> the top.

The girl grimaces and goes back to the typed pages.

19   CLOSE SHOT—TOP OF PAGE ONE OF SCRIPT

CAMERA FEATURES the words "FADE IN."

> GIRL (V.O.)
> Okay . . . What does "Fade In" mean?

20   TWO SHOT—GIRL AND WRITER

> WRITER
> On the dark film a ghost image appears,
> and fades into the first clear picture.
> (beat)
> It's like "The Curtain Rises" at the
> beginning of a stage play. Fade in is always
> capitalized, and lined up against your left-
> hand margin.

She nods and returns to her typed pages.

21   CLOSE SHOT—TOP OF SCRIPT PAGE ONE
This angle features the opening scene of our script, which
reads, "1 EXT. STUDIO ENTRANCE—ESTABLISHING
SHOT—DAY"

> GIRL (V.O.)
> Here's your first typed line. It's in capitals.
> Why?

> WRITER (V.O.)
> That's the scene headline. Every scene in
> your script has a capitalized headline. It
> tells certain vital facts.

CONTINUED

21   CONTINUED

> GIRL (V.O.)
> Is "EXT." a vital fact?

> WRITER (V.O.)
> Indeed it is—to the cameraman, director,
> and production office. It means "Exterior";
> that they are shooting outdoors. But once
> you establish it in a sequence, you don't
> have to repeat it.

> GIRL (V.O.)
> Then you say it's day, and in the same
> scene people are saying "good night" to
> each other.

> WRITER (V.O.)
> It's late afternoon, not dark yet. If there is
> light in the sky, it's "DAY." If no light—it's
> "NIGHT." Once you establish which one,
> you don't have to repeat that either.

> GIRL
> Got it. Final point about the scene headline.
> It's numbered. Why?

22   BACK TO TWO SHOT—WRITER AND GIRL

> WRITER
> Bookkeeping. Every scene in your script
> has a number. The production office
> depends on them to lay out their physical
> shooting schedule. Also, when the film is
> finished, the editor needs them to sort out
> all the short lengths of film.

> GIRL
> You're losing me. What's that got to do with
> writing?

> WRITER
> Nothing. Don't worry about scene numbers
> until you're typing your final shooting
>   (MORE)

CONTINUED

22   CONTINUED

> WRITER
> script. Then number your scenes. It will
> make people think you know what you're
> doing.
>
> GIRL
> (back to script)
> Okay . . . then below the scene headline

23   CLOSE SHOT—SCRIPT
ANGLE FEATURES the scene headline and the descriptive
material directly below.

> GIRL (V.O.)
> You drop a space and go into lower case.
> What's that about?
>
> WRITER (V.O.)
> It's a descriptive of the set, the people, and
> the action the director has to stage. Keep it
> down to essentials; just the facts, brief and
> clear.

CAMERA MOVES DOWN THE SCRIPT PAGE to Scene 2,
where the girl makes her entrance.

> GIRL (V.O.)
> Hey, here I come. Why am I typed in capital
> letters?
>
> WRITER
> The first time any character appears in the
> script, his or her name is typed in caps.

CAMERA MOVES DOWN PAGE to Scene 3 to emphasize
descriptive line, "including her bosom."

24   BACK TO GIRL AND WRITER

> GIRL
> (angrily)
> You old freak, that's chauvinist . . . pigotry!
>
> (MORE)   CONTINUED

24   CONTINUED

> GIRL
> (brandishing script)
> Just cut that line out!

> WRITER
> (patiently)
> We can't. When an important character makes
> her first entrance the writer must give
> the director, the producer, and the casting office a
> thumbnail description. He keeps it quick and
> interesting. Bosoms, bless them, are always
> interesting.

She withers him with a look, but bows to the inevitable and
returns to the script.

25   CLOSE SHOT—SCRIPT SCENE 2
CAMERA MOVES IN to feature the words "BEGIN TITLES
OVER"

> GIRL (V.O.)
> Okay, man . . . what's this "Begin Titles
> Over"?

26   BACK TO TWO SHOT

> WRITER
> The old movies used to begin with big
> printed titles on a black screen. But
> nowadays most feature films and TV start
> on visual teasers, action shots, sometimes
> shock gags.

> GIRL
> Sure they do! They even begin where they
> used to end—in a haystack.

> WRITER
> Right. Here we superimpose our Main and
> Credit Titles on atmospheric shots of you
> casing the studio. The director will select

> (MORE)   CONTINUED

26   CONTINUED

WRITER

picturesque scenes. When the titles are
completed, we simply say "End Titles"—as
in Scene 11, the titles disappear, and we go
on with our story.

GIRL

Wait a minute. Question in Scene 10. What
does "POV" mean?

WRITER

POV means "Point of View." It's a common
camera direction. The camera acts as the
girl's eyes. She reads the plaque which says
"Writer's Building." POV is always typed in
caps.

GIRL

Right ... now we change to his office ...

WRITER
(interrupting)
You mean "we cut." In the final editing
process, the film is physically cut, and the
scenes glued together in continuity. So you
always say we "cut" to the next scene.

27   CLOSE SHOT—SCRIPT SCENE 12
CAMERA FEATURES the scene headline which reads "INT.
WRITER'S OFFICE—FULL SHOT"

GIRL (V.O.)

Here you've got "INT." in caps. Don't tell
me. It means "Interior." Always
abbreviated, and once established, you don't
repeat it.

WRITER (V.O.)

You're catching on.

CAMERA MOVES DOWN descriptive material in Scene 12.

CONTINUED

27 CONTINUED

> GIRL (V.O.)
> You drop a space and describe your set and
> the character. "Writer" is in caps because
> it's his first appearance. He hears a
> "knock." Why is that in caps?

> WRITER
> It is a sound effect. Sound effects, like
> camera directions, are capitalized
> throughout your script.

CAMERA MOVES DOWN script page to pick up the headline
of Scene 13. It reads: "ANGLE FAVORING DOOR."

> GIRL (V.O.)
> What's this "Angle" jive?

28 BACK TO TWO SHOT—GIRL AND WRITER

> WRITER
> "Angle" means the camera's "angle of
> view" . . . what the camera sees and
> photographs.
> (she frowns)
> Do I have to draw you a picture?

> GIRL
> Yes, I'm a dumb broad . . . all bosom . . .
> remember?

He makes a hasty sketch on paper.

29 CLOSE SHOT—SKETCH
The rough sketch illustrates the camera direction "angle."

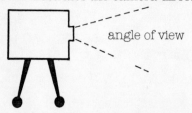

angle of view

CONTINUED

29 CONTINUED

WRITER (V.O.)
"Angle" is purposely a flexible camera
direction. It gives the director wide choice.
He can look through the view finder, and
select his best camera position.

30 BACK TO GIRL AND WRITER

GIRL
Hey, now they start the dialogue. You drop
a couple of spaces, and capitalize the name
of the character speaking. You center their
speeches, and you single space them.

WRITER
Exactly like this page that you are looking
at.

31 CLOSE SHOT—WRITER

WRITER
(significantly)
All these margins, spacings, type sizes, and
indentations approximate script format.

32 CLOSE SHOT—GIRL

GIRL
Loud and clear, Maestro. Will do.
(returns to script)
But what's this?

33 CLOSE SHOT—SCRIPT SCENE 13
CAMERA MOVES IN ON direction which says "She moves to
his desk as they talk, CAMERA ADJUSTING."

GIRL (V.O.)
When she moves to his desk, it says
"Camera Adjusting."

34   BACK TO GIRL AND WRITER

> WRITER
>
> An old-timer taught me that. It simply says
> to the director, "Stage and shoot it the way
> it looks best to you." Some writers prefer to
> say "Camera follows action." Both mean
> about the same thing.

35   MOVING SHOT—SCRIPT SCENE 13
CAMERA MOVES down the script page, stopping momen-
tarily to direct attention to speeches broken up by stage
directions in parentheses.

> GIRL (V.O.)
>
> What's this in parenthesis before the
> writer's speech . . . "reassuringly" . . . ?
> > (beat)
> And farther down in the middle of the girl's
> speech . . . "takes pages"?

> WRITER (V.O.)
>
> Those are stage directions to suggest to the
> director and actor line readings, and bits of
> business.

36   BACK TO GIRL AND WRITER

> WRITER
> > (continuing)
> You type such brief suggestions slightly to
> the left of center, always in parentheses . . .
> on a separate line.

> GIRL
>
> Why?

> WRITER
>
> Because when talkies first started, some of
> the silent actors had never read spoken
> lines of dialogue. When writers put these
> suggestions on the same line—even in
> > (MORE)

CONTINUED

36 CONTINUED

> ### WRITER
> parentheses—a few dumb actors
> memorized the stage directions and read
> them aloud with the dialogue.

> ### GIRL
> Crazy.

She goes back to the script.

37 CLOSE SHOT—SCRIPT SCENE 14
CAMERA CENTERS ON the girl's speech, and the
parentheses "(V.O.)" next to her name.

> ### GIRL (V.O.)
> What's this "V.O."?

> ### WRITER (V.O.)
> It means "Voice over." The audience is
> looking at the screen picture, and hearing
> the girl's voice from off scene. It's usually
> abbreviated or omitted entirely when it's
> clearly understood.

38 TWO SHOT—GIRL AND WRITER

> ### GIRL
> New one in the next scene. You say
> "Individual shot girl." Why?

> ### WRITER
> It means the girl is alone on the screen. It
> gives the director free choice of how to
> photograph her.

> ### GIRL
> But doesn't he use his own judgment
> anyway?

> ### WRITER
> Certainly. And he should That's the
> director's job—to transform your words on

(MORE)   CONTINUED

38   CONTINUED

                    WRITER
        paper to sights and sounds on the screen.
        A good director will give you effects you
        didn't dream of.

                    GIRL
        What about a bad director?

                    WRITER
        Shame on you! There's no such thing.
        When the film is a smash, the director is a
        distinguished artist.
                (pensively)
        If it flops, the director and the actors did
        the best they could with crummy material.

                    GIRL
        Get a grip on yourself, Maestro. I came to
        learn format, not writer's frustrations.

                    WRITER
        Good—you're learning. Most of these
        camera terms explain themselves. I've
        typed a primary list you can keep for
        reference.
                (he gives her typed pages)
        Read them over while I finish the chapter.

                    GIRL
        Thanks.

    She takes the typed sheets. Reading them, she drifts over to
    the couch and sits down.

39   GIRL ON COUCH
    She lies back, reading the typed list. CAMERA PUSHES IN
    TO HOLD the typed page in FULL SCREEN. It reads:

                COMMON CAMERA TERMS
        LONG SHOT (LS)   A scene photographed
                from any considerable distance.

                                    CONTINUED

39 CONTINUED

MEDIUM SHOT (Med Shot or MS)   Midway
between LONG SHOT and CLOSE
SHOT.

CLOSE SHOT   Person or object
photographed to fill or dominate the
screen.

CLOSE-UP (CU)   Usually suggests person
photographed from waist up to full
face.

EXTREME CLOSE-UP (ECU)   Full face or
closer.

FULL SHOT   Taking in most of the set or
scene, as a wide-angle shot inside a
bank.

ESTABLISHING SHOT   Tells you where
you're at. As a LONG SHOT of Eiffel
Tower establishes Paris.

TWO SHOT   Two characters in the scene.

ANGLE FAVORING   The camera is aimed
primarily at any specified character or
object.

AERIAL SHOT or HELICOPTER
SHOT   Camera is airborne, shooting
from a plane or chopper.

CRANE SHOT   Camera is on a mobile arm
or boom. It swings through the air in
any appropriate direction.

FRAME   Any single rectangular picture of
the thousands on a roll of motion-
picture film. "FRAME" is also used,
loosely, for scene or picture, as for
example "Peter enters FRAME." Or
FREEZE FRAME, which means that
the single, identical picture is repeated
over and over.

HIGH ANGLE SHOT   Camera looks down
on scene or person.

LOW ANGLE SHOT   Camera looks up at
same.

PAN SHOT or PANNING SHOT   Comes
from "panorama." The camera is on a

CONTINUED

39   CONTINUED

fixed base, but it swivels its neck, looking either to the right or to the left.

TILT UP or TILT DOWN   Camera looks up, or looks down.

DOLLY SHOT, TRUCKING SHOT, or MOVING SHOT   The camera base is on wheels. It can move on the flat in any direction. Such movement can also be expressed as CAMERA MOVES IN or MOVES BACK; CAMERA DOLLIES IN or DOLLIES BACK, PUSHES IN or PULLS BACK.

SET-UP   A camera position, or a camera angle.

SLOW MOTION   The action is artificially slowed down. As when the lovers come loping lazily through the daisies.

STOCK   Scenes you don't have to shoot, but can buy ready-made from a film library. Such as a St. Patrick's parade down Fifth Avenue, or a long shot of Niagara Falls.

SPECIAL EFFECT(S)   The never-never land of optical illusion. The filming of scenes and phenomena which cannot be realistically staged and photographed. UFOs, ray guns, air armadas, miniatures of sinking ships and bursting dams. The infinite glories of science fiction.

SPLIT SCREEN   The screen is subdivided into two or more scenes of simultaneous action. Typical use is to show both ends of a telephone conversation.

TIGHT SHOT   Exclusive emphasis on specific character or characters. For example, TIGHT TWO SHOT means nothing on the screen but the two of them

CONTINUED

39 CONTINUED

ZOOM SHOT   The camera seems to swoop in from a distance. As in a police lineup scene, when the camera ZOOMS IN on the suspected rapist.

ABBREVIATIONS used in script idiom.

o.s. Off Scene. Usually in lower case letters.

b.g. Background. Usually in lower case letters.

f.g. Foreground (rare). Usually in lower case letters.

V.O. Voice Over. Usually in caps.

POV Point of View. Always in caps.

40 INDIVIDUAL SHOT—WRITER—NIGHT
As he is typing his last page, he realizes that it's getting dark. Without looking around, he reaches for his desk light and turns it on. He checks his closing scene, and types "The End."

WRITER
(pulling page out of machine)
Right, honey, here's the end of the chapter.
(gives her a second look)
Hey, for God's sake!

He gets up quickly, and goes toward her.

41 GIRL ON THE COUCH
She is stretched out full length, her eyes closed. The writer comes into scene, CAMERA ADJUSTING.

WRITER
(shaking her)
Wake up ... !
(harder)
Come on ... get with it!

GIRL
(groggily)
Oh .. hi ... I guess I dropped off.

CONTINUED

41   CONTINUED

> WRITER
> (exasperated)
> But, damn it, you can't fall asleep on me.
> You're the reader!

> GIRL
> (contrite)
> I'm really sorry, Maestro. But this stuff is a
> little draggy . . . all these angles,
> abbreviations . . . definitions.

> WRITER
> (fatalistically)
> Dear child, you are so right. I'm afraid
> there is only one way we can save it.
> (beat)
> Take off your clothes.

The girl sits up indignantly. He pulls down the blinds.

> GIRL
> Like hell I will. I'm a writer, not a sex
> symbol.

> WRITER
> But don't you see . . . this sequence needs a
> gimmick. Something to keep their beady
> little eyes open. You're all I've got!

She gets up from the couch, appealing to him.

> GIRL
> But there are more chapters in the book
> after this. Such a lot about writing that I
> need to know. Can I trust you . . .
> (beat)
> without any clothes . . . for all the rest of
> the pages?

> WRITER
> (paternally)
> Dear child, think back to our earlier pages
> (MORE)

CONTINUED

41   CONTINUED

                         WRITER
              ... to Chapter 5 ...
                         (beat)
              We learn through feeling.

                         GIRL
                         (magnetized)
              Ah, yes ... Chapter 5 ... Content and
              Emotion.
                         (unbuttons her blouse)
              When you're trying to sell them a basic
              lesson ... do it with tears, laughs ...
                         (opens blouse)
              or the old tabasco.

42   CLOSE SHOT—GIRL
      A thought strikes her, as she is peeling off her blouse.

                         GIRL
                         (practically)
              By the way, did you change the scene
              headline from Day to Night?

                         WRITER (V.O.)
              All taken care of.

                         GIRL
                         (dreamily)
              Hey ... I'm learning to be a writer.
                         (takes off blouse)
              Format can be fabulous.
                         (flips blouse away, and looks
                         directly into CAMERA)
              And for all the scripts ever written, here's
              the bottom line. You drop two spaces on
              your right-hand margin, and type in caps ...

                                        FADE OUT

11.

YOUR IDEA FOR A TELEVISION SERIES

And What to Do with It

Everybody has a TV series idea. The lady that lives across the street, neurologists, nuns, and snake charmers. They will swarm around you from the moment that you get your first television screen credit. Forgotten childhood friends will telephone you from North Carolina. Each one has this lock-cinch idea, and all you have to do is turn it into a story, and sell it for them. They will even offer you as much as 50 percent of the proceeds!

Let's face it—those proceeds are generous. The author of a TV series will get perhaps $30,000 for the idea and pilot script. For every episode through all the seasons that the series runs he will receive $750 (or more) as a *creator's fee*. Beyond that, checks will arrive in his mailbox for years of reruns. These latter accrue without his ever bothering to write another line. For the author of a hit series, such proceeds can approach a modest fortune.

The nuns and neurologists all know this. What they don't know is that their precious original idea is scarcely worth the paper on which it is photocopied.

Indeed, there *is* a way to spawn a TV series, beginning with nothing but a bright idea and a ream of blank paper. We will discuss it presently. But first let's demolish, sadly but statistically, this widespread American dream.

The odds against an outsider, or even an unknown struggling writer, cashing in on an "original" series idea are over 1,000 to 1.

A single network, by official estimate, received in one year more than two thousand series presentation ideas. Multiply this by three networks, and a score or more of studios and independent production units. What this blizzard of series ideas totals is anybody's guess. Of all these thousands, perhaps two baker's dozens will actually debut on the air in a given season.

Of these ultimate winners, very few will be truly original. The record shows that networks cling tenaciously to successful formulas. Witness the cloning of the cop shows. We have had young cops and old cops, flatfoots and patrol-car teams, plainclothes and undercover cops, lady cops, S.W.A.T. cops, a cop in a wheelchair, and even a blind detective.

Family shows come in endlessly similar variations. We have had "The Waltons," "The Jeffersons," "Little House on the Prairie," "Father Knows Best," "Eight Is Enough," "Family," "All in the Family," "Family Affair," "One Man's Family," "The Partridge Family," "The Addams Family," and "The Smith Family."

The success of "Roots" spurred a stampede toward the *mini-series*. Most of them are based on published novels or historical material, further restricting original series idea possibilities.

In choosing new series for national broadcast, the networks evaluate more realistic factors than originality. Morton Moss, television editor of the *Los Angeles Herald-Examiner*, reported it this way.

"A well-known producer of prime-time television, who shall be nameless," wrote Moss, "described how a series comes to birth. He mentioned creation with a burst of scarcely controllable mirth.

" 'You decide on what audience you want to hit. Then you decide what ingredients and what kind of characters would interest that audience. You don't create a television series, you engineer it.' "

In the modern media blitz, network executives must be pragmatists. They cannot conduct rash experiments. Not only do they select, for the most part, tested types of material, but they also entrust their series projects to profit-proven producers. Virtually all the new shows are made by established units such as MTM Enterprises, Quinn Martin, Lorimar Productions, Jack Webb, Norman Lear, as well as Universal, Warners, Columbia Pictures Television, and all the major motion-picture studios.

Where do those organizations get their series ideas? Mainly from within their own ranks, or from business associates. Perhaps a powerful agent has interested them in a project or a package. Every producer, writer, and agent in Hollywood knows the fortune that flows from a strategically placed series idea. They know also what time slots are open, and what networks are hungry. All the active producing units have hot "original" ideas of their own to promote with ABC, CBS, and NBC.

These professionals are very sharp males and females. Most of them have come up the hard way. Why should they share their talents and profits with eager outsiders or beginners? Most of them have series ideas of their own that they are trying to get off the ground.

Such practicality may arouse protest. Doubtless, examples can even be found of new series ideas that came from neophytes or nonprofessionals. But the unromantic record will still show that the high percentage is bought from the inside. Let me cite four examples of series ideas conceived and submitted by people from my UCLA writing course. All four were developed with signature characters and a pilot story.

1. Rural flying doctor in the modern West. Based on a living medic, practicing in Utah.
2. Series about a big-city fire station. Written by a career member of the L.A. Fire Department.
3. Family series of mom, pop, and three kids discovering America in a motor home on wheels.
4. A police series about a proposed special weapons and attack team of the Los Angeles Police Department called S.W.A.T.

These four were duly submitted to potential buyers through agents or qualified professionals. Not one, as far as anyone could find out, aroused the slightest practical interest.

Yet four series based on substantially similar ideas were eventually produced and broadcast in prime time.

1. "Doc Elliott," played by James Franciscus, was a series about a flying doctor in today's West.
2. "Firehouse" dramatized the crises and problems of the laddies in a city fire station.
3. "Three for the Road" was a series about a father and his kids cruising America in a mobile home.
4. "S.W.A.T." was a police series about the L.A.P.D. special unit of that name.

No suggestion of plagiarism is here implied or intended. All four of the ideas were basically in public domain. None of the plots or stories bore any similarity to those of the earlier presentations. The eventual creators of the broadcast series doubtless, never heard of the originals. Those lay buried somewhere beneath other thousands of Hollywood's forgotten dreams.

Doubtless, also, there had been *other* proposals on the *same* premises. It is virtually impossible to think of ideas that have not already been submitted by others.

A distinguished professional writer I know spun a series concept out of a state military outfit that functioned years ago along the lawless Arizona border. It had never been publicized, but his uncle had been an officer. The writer flew down to Arizona, tuned in on family connections, and did a lot of privileged research. On his return, the first studio he gave his presentation to told him they already had received formats based on these "Arizona Rangers." At his baffled protest, they checked back. In their files they found over a dozen previous variations of his "original" idea. None of them, incidentally, was ever produced.

All this detail suggests that outsiders are largely wasting their time trying to sell producers or professional writers their series ideas. There *is*, however, one way that any writer—freelance, pro, or eager amateur—can beat the system.

That one way is to write a feature-length special or movie of the week good enough to generate a spin-off.

First requirements are a high-powered story and, above all, a compelling character. That central character (or characters) must be charismatic enough to signature a series or miniseries. Producers and networks have sharp eyes for such screenplays, since good movies of the week are always in short supply. They pay well, too—upwards of $25,000—and they monitor public response to the broadcast closely. If that response is dynamic, the network itself will activate the series.

To be sure, this sounds quixotic, miraculous. Nobody pretends that it's easy. But we will quote briefly from Deanne Barclay, vice-president for NBC's MOWs and mini-series:

"No major supplier can exist on movies of the week alone. We have to think of the series potential on almost every project."

Selling a TV series idea comes down to practical talent and professional clout. Far too much money is at stake for the job to be left to amateurs.

Therefore, if you as an outsider have flashed on a truly striking series character or idea, your one clear chance is to sit down and write it as a pilot screenplay. Copyright it. Any organization that wants to produce that story must buy it from you. In the purchase contract, they must guarantee to give you screen credit and to pay you your creator's fee and residuals as long as the series reruns anywhere on the air.

12.

THE REGULARS IN AN EPISODIC SERIES

A Special Television Writer's Problem

Episodic is Hollywood's trade name for a television series with a central star or group of regulars who head the cast every week. Enduring examples have been "The Waltons," "Columbo," "Gunsmoke," "The Fugitive," "Marcus Welby, M.D." There are a dozen or more such dramatic series on the air every season. This means that there are hundreds of openings for writers to sell original episodic scripts.

A dramatic story for an episodic series poses a special writer's problem

This single star, or these group regulars, are long established—and their character patterns fixed. The audience knows them as old friends, and loves them. They are the series *money*—the special reason that the fans tune in week after week, year after year. The consequences of this are:

1. Their characters are constant. No writer may tamper with them

2. One or more of the regulars must have a major role— or roles—in the script you write

Does that sound over-obvious? Even easy? Wait till you try it. After scores of episodes in any long-running series, it becomes more and more painful to find new entanglements for the same hero or heroine.

The commonest solution is to introduce a brand-new character in your episode with his own special problem for the star or regulars to solve. This often creates its own dilemma. You dream up a good story, a genuinely excellent dramatic idea. But your new character—this for-one-week-only guest star—becomes so interesting that he, or she, robs your regulars of the central spotlight.

Often you won't sell that idea. The first thing that the story editor will say to you is: "That's a damn good story, but our star doesn't have enough to do." Or, "Your dramatic story is not about our series regulars."

Let us note promptly that this requirement is sometimes disregarded. Adventurous producers—like Michael Landon of "Little House on the Prairie"—will experiment with a plot featuring strangers in which his stars are only peripherally concerned. "Police Story" made a practice of it. But when a series has a single star, it is virtually a must that he or she command the spotlight. You cannot, for example, conceive of an episode of "Columbo" without Columbo in the captain's chair.

If a series features several permanent characters ("The Waltons" or "Bonanza"), you do *not* have to star them all every week. But in most episodes, one or more of those regulars must play a pivotal role, or roles.

In practical plot terms, this usually means that the star (and/or regulars) involve themselves in the dramatic problem. They *do not* just stand around giving sage advice, and rerouting emotional traffic. They are not just kibbitzers in the dramatic poker game. Ideally, they should play in it, risking reputation, love, self-respect, or life itself on the turn of the climax card.

A classic example from the five-seasons-long series, "The Fugitive." Dr. Kimble, the star, is fleeing life imprisonment on a false charge of murder. He comes upon a mortally injured child. Because he is a dedicated doctor, he stops to save the child's life. He makes a commitment, and if that commitment goes wrong, he risks the slammer for keeps. He is, thus, totally involved.

Another example from another classic series, "Route 66." For those unborn when it flourished, it was a popular show starring two male sex objects, each with a social conscience. They roared across America in a Corvette, solving cultural problems. In Butte, Montana, they both fell in love with the same girl. But the audience knew she had a terminal illness. The boys didn't know it. By the time they found out, they were totally committed. They were released from that commitment only by her death.

Such love stories are explicit examples. Let's say guest girl wanders into the story with a classic dramatic problem like amnesia. When the star falls in love, then they have a mutual stake in that problem. Perhaps, if it's a western, she's been a hustler in San Francisco, but no one in Poker Flats knows it. When he falls in love with her, our hero's involved.

But be wary of just such stories. The loyal audience of millions knows that the series star cannot get married. A love-of-my-life story has to hit the rocks. They're all ahead of you, which kills the suspense. Accordingly, serious romance can be risky, unless you have a sharp finishing twist for getting Mr. Hero, or Ms. Heroine, out of it before the fade-out.

Another special case. In cop, lawyer, or doctor snows, it is often difficult to involve your star emotionally with the patient, the client, or the bad girl. Perhaps because the doctor or lawyer relationship is, ideally, impersonal. The result is that you can sell a good cop, doctor, or lawyer script even if the hero is not emotionally committed.

But it is better if he or she *is* committed. One favorite

recipe is to put the lawyer, medic, or Angie Dickinson in grave danger of death from the bad guys. Does anyone recall this marvelously moldy old device from some of the earliest TV series? The surgeon hero is grabbed by the heavies and driven to their hideout in the hills. There the Godfather's young brother lies in bed with a bad case of bullet holes. The hero is ordered to operate.

"And if one of you dies, Doc, you both do. Know what I mean?"

In addition to suspense mechanics, most successful producers seek a strong emotional underplot. Witness the experience of two writer friends of mine. Their agent sent them to producers Ivan Goff and Ben Roberts in quest of a script assignment on the popular crime series, "Mannix." The writers pitched two or three ingenious crime gimmicks. Good ideas, but no sale. They were asked back for another conference. Again they came up with some sharp sinful angles. Still Goff and Roberts weren't buying. Finally, they spelled out this basic requirement.

"Forget the crime gimmicks," they said; "those are the easy part. We want a compelling character with a human problem, or a strong emotional relationship. We'll buy that straight off. Then, together, we can work out the crime mechanics in half an hour."

No more practical advice than that could be given to any TV writer—but particularly to writers getting started. Through years of reading story outlines for my UCLA workshop, I found the commonest flaw is lack of audience empathy, personal identification. Most writers strive for a new iniquity, horror, or detective twist, believing that is the first commandment. In quality crime shows, the reverse is true. Flashy plot mechanics are never valid substitutes for human character and emotion. Study a hundred notable crime stories, and you'll find only a handful depending solely on shock or mechanical ingenuity. Classic whodunits are virtually always human stories, skillfully combined with riddle brilliance.

A routine episode of "Kojak" offers a useful sample. A

bedraggled hooker was murdered in the opening. In that first act, and increasingly throughout the story, they made you care about the dead girl—skillfully, unobtrusively. Everybody in the crummy surroundings loved her, including the nail-hard detective Kojak. This was sensitive writing, tough to do without becoming maudlin. The hooker with the heart of gold is among the oldest clichés in fiction. Somebody once said that every male writer has to do that character at least once. But in this "Kojak" they made it work movingly, even though the girl was lost in the first act. It became personally important to every spectator that Kojak expose and convict her killer. Such a human component can be the strongest sales hook you can put into your episodic story.

As final evidence we are going to run down an actual TV episode full length. We've deliberately chosen a remote example that almost no one will remember. It features simplistic values, since they illustrate most clearly the bottom-line essentials. These values include a human problem skillfully mixed with vivid visual action. Note, moreover, that the series star anchors the story line from start to finish.

"The Fire Dancer"

This episode appeared on a series called "Empire." Richard Egan was the series star, as the manager of a vast, modern, Arizona ranch. He was the characteristic strong father figure, who could ride a horse, fly a plane, shoot a bad guy—and yet identify sensibly and personally with human problems.

A spitting torch of flame fills the screen for the opening scene. This is an oil-well fire, blazing out of control. Our hero Egan's problem is to put out the fire before it destroys the ranch's field of oil and gas wells.

He telephones oil fields in Texas for a human extinguisher. Apparently that profession is highly skilled, and a small one. None of the experts is available.

As the burning well blazes hotter, a stranger arrives at the Empire Ranch. With him, in his camper, are an experienced assistant fire-fighter, and a worried wife. The stranger (compellingly played by Frank Gorshin) has heard about Egan's fire, and offers to extinguish it.

Egan mistrusts his credentials. But with the fire running wild, he is forced to the risk. He hires him.

As they inspect the flaming well, the danger mechanics are revealed. A small blast of dynamite will kill the flames for fifty seconds. The stranger and his assistant, in flameproof suits, will go in and put a metal cap on the well. If they fail in those fifty seconds, the fire will reignite and blast them to cinders.

Now we get a private look at the stranger and his wife. He is an extravagant dreamer. He aspires to be the best, as we are all gods or goddesses in our dreams. Moreover, he has brought all the equipment, and he knows all the moves. But he has never actually put out an oil-rig fire before. We realize that he can't face the moment of truth.

So does Egan. But he gets a break. Unexpectedly, the top pro in the oil-well fire-fighting business, an old friend of Egan's, flies in from Texas. He takes over. The stranger is discarded.

But this new expert came alone, and has no assistant. He hires the stranger's old pro partner. They go in together, dynamite the fire, and start to cap the well. But something goes wrong: the cap breaks, the fire erupts and kills them both.

Now Egan, deeply shaken, faces his ultimate dramatic crisis. The blazing well is about to run wild and destroy billions of feet of precious natural gas.

He goes to the stranger's camp. The man and his wife are preparing to pull out when Egan confronts them. The one thing that he knows for sure is that, technically, this stranger understands the job. Egan warns him that if he takes the back road now, he will never be a fire-fighter. He will never be anybody but a guy who ran away from his chance. The wife knows this is true. She joins forces with Egan. Together they persuade him to face the truth, accept the risk.

But one man can't cap the well alone, and his professional

assistant is dead. Egan volunteers to go in beside him. Thus Egan commits himself equally. Now he, too, faces life or death.

They put on the fire suits and go in together. Total suspense, because we have seen that same fire kill two people. They dynamite the flames. They put the cap on the well, twist it down tight. Success. The fire is out!

Thus Egan risks his life to resolve a crisis. In addition, he treats a human problem. He brings the stranger to grips with himself and reality. The man's wife knows what it means to their future—and so does the audience.

Perhaps such a story pattern may seem a bit primitive to sophisticates and modernists. Indeed, it was. It dramatized one of the deepest of human emotions—fear in the presence of death. It combined, as all good movies should, the visual with the visceral. The episode was written by Alvin Sargent, who won an Academy Award in 1977 for his screenplay of *Julia*. We could all prosper cordially writing that kind of primitive.

13.

SITUATION COMEDY

For sheer craftmanship, some of our leading sit-coms are the best-written TV in town. This viewpoint may induce internal rising and active nausea in the few heavy thinkers who have come this far. Particularly since I have never written a situation comedy. Comedy, yes ("Maverick," "The Rogues") but sit-coms, no. Thus, I can't possibly know what I'm talking about.

But I have a useful plus going for me. Of all types of prime-time TV, sit-coms are the most consistently guided by writers. This is in signal contrast to many dramatic shows and "specials," which are so often riddled with executive incompetence.

Norman Lear, Allan Burns, Jim Brooks, and most of the sit-com top bananas began as writers. Except for inevitable network interference, there are practically no noncreative masterminds at sit-com story conferences. Virtually all the executive producers, producers, executive story editors, consultants, etc., are actually in-house writers. Lurking under those heady titles, they collaborate on most of the program's shows. From hundreds of sit-coms they have put together, they know their exacting craft.

Consult your own rating system. You may not even like sit-coms. Yet most of you will agree that the good ones are more skillful to their purpose than much of the "dramatic" junk that surrounds them in prime time. We need only cite two significant examples: "All in the Family" and "M*A*S*H." No dramatic series in the same years compares to them.

That type of situation comedy is the backbone of the trade. Since I had never written sit-coms myself, I applied to some established pros for some craft mysteries, guidelines, and common sense.

They denied any mysteries. They all agreed on a simple keystone for getting laughs. It is blood kin to the essence of deepest tragedy. Human characterization.

But where have we heard that before? We've heard it over and over in these chapters, until it is becoming our most insistent cliché. We certainly won't run through it all again. We will just point to two enduring examples of situation comedy through human characterization—Archie Bunker and Ted Baxter.

What any aspiring writer need bear in mind is one fundamental fact. Effective comedy is not based on mechanical gimmicks. The banana peel isn't funny. It is the character who slips on it that gets you your laughs.

Story Hook Idea

Pick your story idea from this same human character tree. Most good sit-coms kick off on a wacky character predicament. Like an old one from "The Mary Tyler Moore Show." Basic to Mary's characterization, you'll recall, was her lack of a steady love object. So they gave her one, a mysterious, persistent, love-smitten admirer. When he arrived on screen about halfway through, he turned out to be fourteen years old.

When I asked about originality in character story hooks, I got looks of indulgent disbelief. My mentors explained patiently that there are no brand-new character angles. Old-timers know them all. Originality lies in your knack of relating the character glitch to the unique personality in the series. Prejudice, for example, is a human failing older than comedy itself. How the unique personality of Archie Bunker exemplifies prejudice has made a landmark TV series.

The predicament on which you base your story should be

human and very real. The actors in a successful series are funny people. They will generate laughs by responding to that predicament in their unique, comedic way.

Finally, the basic character dilemma should not be long delayed. My pro adviser recommended that you set up your plot idea in the first couple of pages. At this, time doubled strangely back for me.

Years ago, before television had installed footlights in all our living rooms, I was talking with Arthur Ripley, a leading writer, producer, director, about the techniques of Mack Sennett comedies. These were, of course, the classic prototypes of off-the-wall screen humor. Ripley recalled Mack Sennett himself storming into a story conference one day, shaking a script under his gagmen's (writers') noses. He yelled at them that if they wanted to stay on his payroll, they'd better tell the audience what their goddamn story was about by the top of the second page.

Sit-Com Structure

After this practically instant opening on a wacky character crisis, your design structure for a sit-com is basically this:

The focal character struggles furiously to get out of his predicament. The harder he struggles, the more he screws himself up. This technique, of course, is blood kin to the classic complications of the three-act design (Chapter 1). In both drama and comedy, the complications reach their peak point of no return at the second-act climax.

In sit-coms this structure is similar, but concentrated. Most of them run only a half hour, and must be crafted for commercial breaks at fixed points. Their story smashup (second-act climax) comes at the halfway point, just before the middle commercial. The audience is left breathless and hanging to watch that commercial. In the concluding minutes of your story, you rescue your character from the debris of his climax disaster.

Suspense and Conflict—Tried and True

Conflict and suspense are your unfailing adjutants in comedy, as they were in drama. Without character conflict, for example, comedy could scarcely exist. These obvious contributions are detailed in Chapters 3 and 4.

The essential difference in their applications lies in the characters' reactions. In serious drama, conflict and suspense exist in earnest. In sit-coms, offbeat character attitudes make them play for laughs.

The Dialogue Contrast

Along with similarities come compelling distinctions between dramatic and sit-com techniques. Most conspicuous is the dialogue factor.

A great dramatic situation, as we've discovered, can rivet your audience with spare and unobtrusive dialogue. In fact, a major crisis can be played in monosyllables, or even silence. But the lifeblood of most sit-coms is their constant flow of laugh lines. A good dialogue script provides a laugh every ten or fifteen seconds. Norman Lear, high priest-producer in the sit-com field, has said, "We live or die from line to line."

Of special importance is the stinger on the tail of every act or scene. This carries vital story interest forward on the irresistible wave of a big laugh.

Vive La Difference

The sharply significant difference between broad comedy and straight drama seems to be the cockeyed angles that sit-com characters take to their story predicaments. When "the family" does not realize how grave their crisis is—but the audience does—then the situation becomes automatically funny.

For example, sister discovers a plastic blob in the living room. It seems to be ticking faintly. In serious drama, the frightened cast would identify it as a time bomb, and get rid of it at instant risk to their lives. But comedy characters are clothed in a divine immunity. They pass the little blob around wonderingly, listening to it, shaking it, discussing it earnestly. Mother tests it by dropping it in the tank with their beloved tropical fish. Smoke hisses from the tank, and the fish flip out all over the rug. The blob continues ticking, but the family members—still unaware of disaster—scramble to rescue the fish instead of themselves.

Certain Practical Aspects

Little that you get prodigally paid for in show business is easy. Especially writing. But sit-com writing has one clear advantage over writing for dramatic film and TV. You don't have to earn a major-league paycheck the first time you come to bat. You can develop your skills. There are comedy minor leagues where any writer can test out his prospective talent.

Scores of thousands of sketches, gags, and one-liners are burned up every season by stand-up comics, night club acts, talk show hosts, public appearances, roasts, and variety shows. Good jokes are in incessant, overwhelming demand.

Contact procedures are seldom formidable. Go to your local night spot, or anywhere in your city or county where comics work. Don't be bashful; find out what they need. Address more exalted comedians by mail, directly, or through their agents. Provide a résumé, if you have written anything, anywhere, for anybody. Include some brief, punchy material that you think suits a particular comic's delivery.

When you receive an encouraging response send in a couple of dozen one-liners. If he—or she—buys three or four at about ten bucks apiece, you're a pro comedy writer.

It is still a long jump from the local radio station to the flesh and jackpots of Southern California. When you have made a few modest scores, the practical kick is to come on out here. Unknown gag writers *have* been hired by mail, but only the tiny few with instant, unforgivable talent. Experiences of my students recommend an old, old technique. Standing outside the door, screaming and beating on it with hands and feet, is the only scientific method of breaking it down.

Outline vs. Screenplay

When you force the first crack in the door, you must have a script ready to shove through it. Choose a sit-com that you really like. You'll write it better.

You may do well, also, to choose a story situation with some substance beneath those staccato dialogue laughs. Modern sit-com producers are increasingly in search of content. Witness the subject of rape, as treated on "All in the Family." As we noted in Chapter 5, "Content and Emotion," some of the finest and funniest sit-coms are fiercely satirical. They are *about something*. We suggest that you cut back to that earlier chapter. It explores such essential factors in detail.

Whatever series you choose, absorb the characters. Remember that what interests the producer is his "family." An outside personality should never wander in and dominate the story—never. If you're writing a script for a female star, the story crisis must be the star character's, not her orthodontist's.

A few experts will tell you to write and submit a story outline, or breakdown. Most of those that I talked to said the hell with that. All a sharp outline proves is that you can write an outline. A producer needs a working script.

What he wants to know most of all is—do you understand and can you write his characters. Make them jump off the pages at him. Include sight gags, and plenty of laugh lines. *You must be funny on paper!* Your gags, character punch lines, and stingers are what get read. They alone can pull you through the producer's door.

Sit-Com Special Format

You should be as professional as possible in your script presentation. Producers are harassed and busy people. They are also experts, with little time and patience for bumpy inexperience.

The format of sit-com scripts is somewhat different from the standard film and TV setup (illustrated in Chapter 10). The most obvious difference lies in double spacing of dialogue, and sometimes of stage directions. Since laugh lines are the guts of the process, a sit-com script takes a lot of that double-spaced dialogue. Therefore their scripts go longer in page count. A half-hour sit-com script may run as long as fifty pages.

Other minor differences are too technical to investigate here. Buy, beg, or steal a professional sit-com script. You will find plenty floating around Hollywood. A thoughtful read-through will teach you how to put your script down on paper in standard professional form.

Waiting Pains

Once your script is on the producer's desk, you face the ultimate predicament. It haunts all writers in every medium. Sweating out the verdict.

Remember Dorothy Parker's immortal description of a Hollywood writer. He settles down at his desk, puts a fresh sheet of paper in his typewriter, "and sits there waiting for the phone to ring."

Break the pattern. The only pill for waiting pains is to start work on your next story idea.

That final verdict is rarely quick in coming. For newcomers, my class experience shows that sit-coms are more demanding, more resistant than most dramatic series. My best-ever student in comedy writing took some three years of constant, stubborn writing before she was offered a program staff job. That meant that she had finally cracked the unyielding magic circle.

Any professional sit-com writer will tell you why. On most scripts for most series, the writing process is stormy and gregarious. Scripts are written, revised, rehashed, and constantly rewritten by all those staff editors, producers, and consultants. In chronic crisis, they may work twenty-four hours at a stretch. Under urgent conditions, they are inclined to hire their friends, people they know and trust. To become known and trusted, strangers must offer panic-proof dispositions, along with proven comedy skills.

Perseverance

While waiting for the magic break, smart tyros take jungle training. They attend courses and seminars, particularly those conducted by professional comedy writers. They make friends and establish vital contacts. Sometimes they acquire collaborators. Programs often encourage writing teams. Say a staff job is worth $1,600 weekly. Most producers are happy to get two writers for the price of one.

Professional training schools for comedy writers are on the drawing boards. At Twentieth Century-Fox a small band of recruits is being processed from all over the country. They are hired on the basis of submitted work, and will be paid while training and learning. Workshops in writer development hark back to bygone years at MGM and other major motion-picture studios. Such in-studio training can be richly productive. But it requires instructive intelligence. It also costs the parent studio significant money. Whether it proves itself in modern TV profit columns, only time will tell.

Cash Considerations

Prices in the slapstick supermarket are glossy. For a half-hour sit-com script, a solo writer earns upwards of $6,000. When that episode reruns in the summer, he receives a second $6,000. But term staff jobs are the backbone of the craft action. Those in-house writers, executives, editors, producers, creative consultants make from $1,500 to $15,000 a show, throughout the series season. Highest prices of all go for the pilot scripts for new series. Such an original may earn the creator as much as $30,000.

In addition, all writers who receive screen credit on any

episode of any show collect residuals. Those are royalties won for their members by the Writers Guild, and described in Chapter 15. They are cash returns paid again and again (on a declining scale) as long as the writer's show replays anywhere on the air. A sit-com writer with multiple credits on a couple of hit series can lie back and rest easy for some time to come.

Words in Parting

Comedy writers are often specially sensitive people. They have to be to spot the invisible difference between the comic and the stupefying cliché. Seasoned pros, who contributed to this research, were all trying to tell us (writer-reader) one essential thing. They didn't want to seem too assured, and they didn't want to make us look stupid. They were expressing the simple secret of rough-and-tumble or of dialogue comedy writing. That is that you had better be born funny.

This seems so chokingly obvious that it ought to be taken for granted, or perhaps just left out. But I *must* include it. Because every writer, and just about everybody else you know, is truly convinced that he has an inspired sense of humor.

Let's illustrate, as we've done before, in reverse. Each season, network millions are spent on so-called *comedy dramas,* or romantic comedy "specials." A boss with more clout than comedic instinct hires writers, a director, and actors who are not all crazybone geniuses. Working earnestly together, they produce the worst of television's mighty array of miserables—the long, dogged comedy that dies trying.

An uninspired drama can get by on a tangle of clichés, expertly played by gifted actors, winding up with a fifty-block car chase. But a gawky, fumbling comedy that fights a two-hour losing battle for laughs is an embarrassing disaster.

Yet such things keep on happening. Because next to nobody—in or out of show business—accepts the grim fact that a true gift of comedy is God-given to only the cherished few.

Before you try to write (or produce, or direct) comedy on

a professional level, be very sure that you share that gift. Is your material constantly and truly funny? Not just to yourself and your six-year-old daughter, but to the cold and dirty world around you. Can you really make people laugh?

If you can, then don't hesitate to risk the first rough years. To offer an audience flashes of your own private lunacy, and to hear them respond in joyous laughter—that is among the great rewards of the writing experience.

14.

AGENTS

The Common Sense of Getting One

Everyone in the talent field in films and television has an agent. Why?

You need a sales agent for your scripts and services just as you need a real-estate agent when you have a house to sell. Because he knows who and where the buyers are. He knows the market, the prices, and the pitfalls.

You can't get on the telephone, or go from door to door selling your house. Equally, you can't go plugging around town to producers' offices or keep calling them on the phone about your literary epic. You don't even know the names of all the producers in this sprawling city.*

To be sure, in preparation at this writing are the early issues of a reliable directory. Called *The Scriptwriter's Marketplace*, it is projected by the oldest of the local film daily papers, *The Hollywood Reporter*. It gives the vital statistics of all active film and TV producers, programs, studios. Significantly, the

---

* This chapter deals with the agent question for readers and writers in the Hollywood area. Advice on agent procedures for those living elsewhere will be found in the next chapter.

bottom line of almost every producer's entry is this: "Submissions accepted through agents only."

Reputable and recognized agents get a 10 percent commission on every job they get you, and on every script they sell. This is a standard fee in the industry, the same commission that is paid by actors, producers, and directors. The agents have an association open only to qualified professionals. All their members are known to and approved by the Writers Guild.

Generally speaking, most reputable agents do not demand payment for services in advance.

A good agent is not easy to get—for beginners. You will find that the major offices have a full list of clients. Many agents begrudge the time that it takes to market a new name, since film producers prefer to buy writers with track records and screen credits. But if you can write a skilled script, you should have no real trouble. Talented clients are an agent's lifeblood.

If the prospect disconcerts you, remember that every one of the thousands of members of the Writers Guild started with a stack of blank paper and no agent. So how do you go about getting one?

Approach Shots

The best way, like the best approach to most business projects, is to know someone who will give you a recommendation. Like a writer friend who will take your script in to his own agent. Or a shaggy old uncle who owns a movie studio.

Lacking those things, drive down to the Writers Guild at 8955 Beverly Boulevard. Ask at the desk for a copy of their list of accredited agents. It costs $1.00. Usually the current list includes entries with stars in the margin. This means that they will read material from new or nonmember writers. Go home, call up, and say you have a manuscript to submit for consideration. Keep calling until you have found one who will read it.

But—and this is all-important—do *not* call an agent until you have a finished script, or at least a detailed, constructive outline. It must be work into which you have put your best effort—and it must be *good!* Few agents are altruists or breast-feeders. They are in the film business to make money, not to supply a social service.

If you bother an agent to read a manuscript that is incomplete or amateurish, he won't even finish it. He certainly won't want to read anything of yours in the future. Your first chance to get him interested is your best chance.

Submit clean, sharp copy. If the work is patched or foggy (worn ribbon or sloppy corrections), it is hard to read, and sets up sales resistance. Use a typewriter with Pica type or larger. Always double space an outline. Neat, legible pages create a positive impression.

If you have ever been paid for writing anything, include a résumé. Publication, any professional writing employment, or bylines add credibility. Keep it mercifully short.

Okay—you've got a great story, a complete outline or script, flawlessly typed, and you have located an agent who will read a new writer's material. Hand-carry it to his office. Introduce yourself to his secretary, who might possibly send you in to see him. That'll be the day. Just leave your script, go home, and wait.

One of the miseries of the business is the time it takes to get a reading on all but high-urgency scripts. There are always extenuations. Producers and agents have broad demands on their reading time. The only thing an eager new writer can do is to call in to the agent's secretary every week or ten days. With luck the agent will be reminded.

Finally, a report comes back. If he has read it and likes it, you've got an agent. If he turns you down, continue the process with another agent on the Guild list. If the work is competent and commercial, someone will spark to it.

This is a dreary, grueling process. There are quicker methods. I have known a student to bounce into a major agent's office, spin a cheerful commercial, and leave with a firm agreement. Agents are master pitchmen; they respect the smarts. A noted agent has said he would rather represent a super-salesman than Shakespeare. The hustler will work more often. If God gave you any special sales skill, don't neglect it. Hollywood is a make-believe ballroom, where gifted people haunt the sidelines because good agents never asked them to dance.

15.

SALES PROCEDURES

Top and Bottom Dollar

In presenting your film or television script for sale, it helps to be a mind reader. Because some agents and producers prefer a script in full screenplay form. Others argue conclusively that the outline or treatment is the only way to go.

The Outline or Treatment

Developing your dramatic story in outline or treatment form is much like condensing it into a prose short story, told in the present tense. For a one-hour TV episode this outline might run ten or fifteen pages. Type those pages on standard 8½ by 11 bond paper, double spaced, with generous margins.

If your story is for a movie or TV special, your outline may cover thirty to seventy pages. Garrulous writers on epics can double or triple that. Don't ape them; excess length makes deadweight. The virtue of an outline or treatment is that it is quicker to write, and to read.

I am often asked just what the word *treatment* means, and where it came from. It was coined in the ancient days when producers first bought stage plays and novels for their silent movies. A novel that ran four or five hundred pages presented problems, including the fact that it would run half the night. A one-set stage play just wasn't a movie. It had to be chased outdoors, and activated.

Trained screenwriters were hired to revamp these materials. Their problem was how to "treat" the play or novel to make it into a silent movie. They synopsized their ideas for the producer in narrative form, and in the present tense. This adaptation outline was known as the treatment.

Treatment vs. Screenplay

Certain agents warn you firmly that producers are too busy to read full screenplays from new writers. They say they can judge the story's merit from the outline or treatment. This makes practical sense to all except producers and story editors who deny it. They, in turn, say that they have bought too many gold bricks, with flashy surface ideas, but shabby substance beneath. The only way really to tell, they contend, is to read a full script. Then the characters and the dialogue either come to life or drop dead.

After years of such conflicting convictions, I ran a practical test. I checked the actual sales experience of recent students. I found that their completed scripts had made them more money than their treatments or outlines.

Why?

Penny-wise, producers have a disconcerting way of trying to buy a student writer's idea, but not the writer. Perhaps they offer him $800. He's flattered, he's hungry, he sells. Then the producer calls in a seasoned professional and pays him thousands to do the shooting script.

The producer's logic is unassailable. He knows that his experienced writer will deliver a shootable screenplay. The inexperienced student may fall flat on his pads. "We are not" (how many times have I heard this when recommending a student) "running a school for writers."

Prolific students have asked me if it's possible to make a living just selling story ideas. It is not. Prices paid for outlines and story ideas are much smaller (roughly one-third) than those for screenplays. No writer that I ever heard of made his living just peddling original outlines.

Screenwriters earn their keep, big or little, writing screenplays. Those determined to join the club should prove early that they can put together shooting scripts. Those are written in the special format, almost identical for films or filmed television, which was fully detailed in Chapter 10.

Such a complete screenplay is a far greater challenge than an outline. It involves more time and more hard work. The beads of blood on your forehead get bigger. But no producer can give you the cold eye and claim that you can't write a working script if you have laid such a script on his desk. Furthermore, a sympathetic producer—and there are many—will be far more receptive to a writer who has put all that creative effort into a script for his program.

Still the producer may feel, perhaps justifiably, that it needs work. Almost all original scripts do, including those by experienced writers. If he wants to proceed with the project, he must still buy your concept. He will probably pay you more for it than he would for a twelve-page outline.

Length of Television Scripts

Producers sometimes check the last page of a newcomer's teleplay before they read the first. How long is it? Weird lengths make them apprehensive.

Standard lengths, give or take a few pages, are these: for a one-hour dramatic series show, your script in standard format should run about 60 pages; your script for an hour-and-a-half show, about 90 pages; and your script for a two-hour show, about 120 pages.

Extended scripts for dramatic two-parters, or for the longer form mini-series, can be estimated on roughly the same scale. As you have probably noticed, it reckons out at about one typed script page to one minute of tube time.

There is one maverick exception to this general pattern.

Situation comedy—what else? Sit-coms fill half-hour time slots. Their shooting scripts have a somewhat specialized format, including double-spaced dialogue (see Chapter 13, "Situation Comedy"). Sit-com scripts, for each half-hour episode, run around 45 to 50 pages.

Length of Feature Film Scripts

Screenplay lengths for feature films are more flexible. Write as many pages, within sensible limits, as you need to tell your tale effectively. The "page a minute" yardstick does not apply, since theatrical showings are not chopped up and retarded by commercials.

Your shooting script for the usual program picture should come in comfortably at around 125 to 140 pages. Thinner than that, it may seem to a producer-purchaser like a TV play. Much fatter, it might suggest a bloated budget.

Multimillion-dollar epics, which run two hours and more in the theater, require longer scripts, 200 pages and up. Those are always written by expensive and experienced pros.

Copyright—Guild Registration

Writing a complete screenplay offers a practical fringe benefit. You can copyright it.

The red tape is minimal. First write a note requesting Registration Form D—Dramatic Composition to:

Register of Copyrights
Copyright Office
Library of Congress
Washington, D.C. 20559

They will send you Form D, plus a request for $6.00. Fill out their form, and mail it back with your script and your money. You will receive a certificate of formal copyright.

Copyright protects a literary work from the date of issue until fifty years after the author's death.

Note well, however, that the copyright law covers only completed manuscripts "ready for presentation or performance." It *excludes* titles, ideas, outlines, synopses, or treatments. To plug this gap, the Writers Guild has set up its own registration service. Any writer can register his outline or treatment for a feature film, or his format idea for a television series or story. The fee for nonmembers is $10.00. Apply to the Writers Guild* for forms and procedure.

Life in California

Okay, you have completed your first screenplay and applied for copyright. What is your next essential step?

You must get an agent. Many studios, networks, and producers will not even read scripts from unknown writers. For those of you who live in Southern California, the whole matter of agents has been considered in Chapter 14.

If you live elsewhere in the country, however, you've got a problem. You have to write to the Writers Guild of America, West. Ask for their list of accredited agents, and enclose $1.00. This list covers the whole country. Certain agents are identified as interested in reading the work of new writers. Query them, including a brief résumé of your professional writing background, if any. When you get a positive response, forward your script. Then sit back and wait. It may take many weeks.

To be sure, you can also mail your manuscript blindly to a network, studio, or individual producer. We all believe in miracles, like the one about the sympathetic producer who reads a new writer's script and sends back his check for thousands, plus airfare to Los Angeles. We also hear of a beauty

* Writers Guild of America, West
8955 Beverly Boulevard
Los Angeles, California 90048

Writers Guild of America, East
22 West 48th Street
New York, New York 10036

queen "discovered" from a lucky photograph. Or a child actor plucked squealing from a little theater group in Tulsa, Oklahoma. Those miracles *do* happen. But they happen to only one dreamer in a hundred thousand whose hopes are pitched toward Hollywood.

For practical dreamers, there are way stations. Constant film activity in New York offers writing opportunities. Television stations in many cities support local production units. Writers are needed for news, commercials, special announcements, etc. The late Rod Serling was one of the most successful TV writer-producers of all time. He worked two years at a hinterlands television station before selling his first script to a national network show.

Universities, colleges, and schools in many states have expanding departments of cinema. Youngest of the arts, it has become a vital cult. The cornerstones of college programs are courses in screenwriting. Many include actual production. More and more of their graduates are coming out to California to put their talents to the acid test.

But not everybody is privileged to earn university credits in cinema, or get a training job at a midwestern TV station. If you're writing on your own, the long wait to get an agent interested—let alone a studio or network—can be deeply dispiriting. It may put a frantic idea in your head—frantic, but strangely practical:

"If I'm that hooked on writing films, why not go to California?"

Virtually every successful film and TV writer plies his trade in and around Hollywood. For a basic reason. Writing a movie script is rarely an ivory-tower interlude. It is an adventure in confrontations.

Since the earliest days, the story conference has been the guts of the creative process. As your script develops, you have to confer constantly with your producer, story editor, director, and network people.

You have to keep in close touch with your agent and writer friends to monitor the market. You have to read the two daily bibles of the industry, *The Hollywood Reporter* and *Variety*, to know who's doing what to whom, and who's getting paid. You have to live in California to make contacts and have lunch, to have meetings, have tennis, sex, sailing, and hangovers. In short, to have life as it is lived by most working film writers.

Nothing herein should suggest that the act of coming to the West Coast will make you a writer. The very concentration of job seekers intensifies the competition. Getting on the industry payroll takes talent, luck, overwork, and usually three or four years of your life.

Meanwhile you have to exist. It might be of some comfort to know that the *Los Angeles Times* has one of the largest Sunday want-ad sections in the world. Many of the nonprofessional students in my UCLA course are driving taxis or typewriters, selling threads, or slinging hash while hustling to unload that first TV or filmscript.

George Orwell (*1984*) spoke of authorship as an exhausting struggle. He said that "one would never undertake it, if one were not driven by some demon he could neither resist nor understand."

Are you driven by that demon? Only in California will you find your true brothers and sisters. That is where the action is. That is where a stranger first begins to sense the cries and the smells of the marketplace.

Professional Price Tags
Top and Bottom Dollar

There are some five thousand members of the Writers Guild of America, West. These are the professionals who turn out 90 percent or more of the scripts for feature films and prime-time television.

The annual income of all these smoking pens approximates $100 million. This averages out at around $20,000 per writer. But, of course, average has nothing to do with it. Scores of strugglers moonlight at other jobs, and count themselves lucky to make one TV sale a season. Almost half the membership hovers below the $10,000 level. Conversely, the torrid top 8 percent make $75,000 and on up, apiece.

Actual figures, as quoted in the Guild *Newsletter* for September 1978, were these:

INCOME	% OF REPORTED WRITERS
Up to $2,000	21.9
$2,000–$4,000	10.7
4,000–10,000	17.8
10,000–15,000	8.0
15,000–20,000	7.4
20,000–25,000	4.6
25,000–50,000	13.8
50,000–75,000	7.8
75,000 or more	8.0

Television Dollars

Fees for writing most television series scripts are fixed by agreement between the Writers Guild and the networks and producers. The Guild is an open-membership labor union to which every established writer must belong. Networks and producers can hire only Guild members to write their scripts, and must pay them Guild minimums, or better.

The schedule of fees is wildly complicated, and changes every season—for reasons too complex to consider here. The following figures are valid approximations for 1979. Barring economic disaster, they will certainly rise in subsequent years.

For his story and screenplay a qualified television writer will be paid:

$6,000 for a half-hour series episode
$8,000 for a one-hour series episode
$12,000 for an hour-and-a-half show
$16,000 for a two-hour show

Most of these series episodes will be repeated during the summer reruns. The writer receives a 100 percent residual payment for that rerun. Which is a long way of saying that he gets paid in full a second time.

He also receives residual payments, on a descending scale, for reruns in subsequent seasons. To be sure, many of the less distinguished shows do not go on to multiple repeats. But the true durables ("M*A*S*H," "Gunsmoke," "The Mary Tyler Moore Show") pay their writers lavish residual totals over many years.

In addition, the writer receives a suitable, but varying, slice of the producer's gross for foreign telecasts.

Certain weekly programs employ staff, or in-house, writers. This is especially true of comedy series and variety shows. The Guild minimum wage for such opulent slavery is around $900 a week. Specially talented staff writers are in demand for double or triple that.

The highest prices in television are paid for two-hour specials, for pilots, for movies of the week, and for the dramatic mini-series, which run over several weeks. Their writers drag down from $15,000 to $50,000.

Such sums may sound unreal to working folk, teachers, salespeople, secretaries, bus drivers. So are the paychecks of star athletes and distinguished head shrinkers. Television is not just a plush creative ghetto; it is an intensely exacting craft. Most writers who take home the big money are reliable, master craftsmen and women. Television is also the world's weirdest combination of crap table and freak show. It helps to be a super-conperson, or just plain shot with luck.

Feature Film Fees

The most successful television writers soon move up to the highest rent district of all, which is feature theatrical films. The numbers are dizzying. For writing the scripts of major pictures, the fees to important "name" writers may run $200,000—and up.

To be sure, lesser-budget movies are made, and the sums paid to the writers are much smaller. Minimums still exist, since the Guild takes a dim view of any writer getting ripped off. Here again, to quote precise figures is impractical, since they can only grow as time goes by and inflation goes up. Let's say that for a story and screenplay of the most modest film, the market bottoms out at around $12,000.

For medium-budget films there is no valid yardstick. A widely respected agent estimates that the original story and script for a film budgeted at $1 million should sell for $50,000, and probably more.

If the writer and his agent can interest a major star or a leading director in their script, the price multiplies magically. William Goldman, author of *Butch Cassidy and the Sundance Kid*, using that method, received what was reported as the highest price ever paid for an original story and screenplay, $400,000. Sterling Silliphant (*The Poseidon Adventure*, *The Towering Inferno*) is headlined in *Variety* as having signed with Warner Brothers to write three scripts for over $1 million, plus a percentage of profits. Neil Simon and Paddy Chayefsky write their habitual hits for fees plus percentages that surely sum up in the millions.

These are extraordinary totals, earned by writers of extraordinary talents. For every one of those, there are hundreds wandering around Hollywood, wondering where their next assignment is coming from. Drifting down the same streets are undiscovered actors, actresses, directors, producers. They, too, face fame or famine.

The manufacture of films and television is often described as an industry. But for those who write, direct, produce, or star in big hits, it is an inspired insanity. The projected $250 million gross of *Star Wars* suggests that even the sky is no longer the limit. It is nudging outer space.

16.

GRAB BAG

Angles, Knacks, and No-Nos

Every professional you work with in films or television has strong personal convictions about the reasons scripts play or flop. Some are selfishly guarded secrets. Some are folk wisdom you might pick up from the prop man on the set. Most practical writers will compare notes, listen, and share. Because the smallest suggestion from someone who knows his craft may decide the fate of a scene, a characterization, or indeed a total project.

Pointers from Howard Hawks

Let's start with Howard Hawks, who has certainly won his permanent Director's Chair in the Film Pantheon. I picked up three practical pointers while writing the script for *Tiger Shark*, in which he directed Edward G. Robinson. Hawks was the ultimate pragmatist about film writing and directing. From making many pictures, he had found that certain things worked for audiences, and others didn't. That was all he knew or cared.

Hawks liked to open any scene—when he sensibly could—with a character entrance. He felt that the visual entrance relieved the stiffness of a standing start. His second point was to keep at least one character on his feet through any dialogue scene. "When everybody sits down," said Hawks, "your scene is liable to sit down with them." Finally, he counseled: "Don't tell me what kind of character your girl is. Show me by what she does."

From Owen Davis

Owen Davis once pointed out to me two probable paths to disaster that seem to have escaped common notice. One or more of them bobs up every season or so, and costs its investors bitter millions. And just who—I can hear the murmurs rising—was Owen Davis?

Davis was probably the most prolific playwright in the history of the American theater. When I interviewed him for a Sunday newspaper story, even he couldn't say precisely how many plays of his had been produced. Legend puts it at over two hundred, beginning with juicy melodramas like *Her One False Step* and ending with his Pulitzer Prize winner, *Icebound.*

Davis's first warning was against a full cast sheet of bad guys. Take care not to crowd your screen with repugnant characters. This is an easy mistake to make in a violence melodrama. Be sure that you balance all those bad guys with a character or two whom your audience can accept in good comfort. From some bitter experience, Davis had learned that a theater audience becomes uneasy when wholly surrounded by hostiles. As you or I would if caught for a couple of hours in the crowded exercise yard of San Quentin prison.

Davis's second caution flag was against piling too much agony on a helpless character. Sounds logical, you say; seems obvious. It eludes the writers, directors, and financial backers of the multimillion-dollar bombs of almost any season. A helpless character means anyone that can't fight back—a child, an older or handicapped person, a wife in love and unable to defend herself against a sadistic husband. Davis had found that the audience will identify with the helpless character and be unable to endure his or her protracted torment.

The remedy to both these problems lies in relief and contrast. A modern instance would be *A Patch of Blue*, in which the helpless character was the blind daughter of a sodden prostitute, played by Shelley Winters. Shelley hated her, beat her up physically, and threw her downstairs. No vicarious agony can exceed watching a blind person taking blows she cannot see. The audience would not have endured that child's torment through a whole running. But the film was a deserved success. Because they relieved the girl's suffering with escape trips. In the city park outside, she found a voice of understanding and refuge—Sidney Poitier's. Throughout the story he provided crucial relief and contrast. Plus suspense, because she couldn't see he was black.

Remembering Joseph Conrad

When classic novels were in their glory, Joseph Conrad described his personal reasons for writing fiction. He said that his aim was to make you, the reader, "feel and know what I feel and know. But most of all, I want to make you see it."

Conrad never wrote a movie, but his observation could be the starting gun for any scriptwriter.

Old Guard Heroes

Nothing is more significant about modern movie concepts than the maturing of heroes. The old machos—Errol Flynn, Clark Gable—believed in big business, virtuous women, and Almighty God. Humphrey Bogart sired a new breed of iconoclasts. Your modern, realistic heroes, such as Redford, McQueen, Nicholson, are not just watchdogs of truth. They are seekers after it.

Motivation

No word is more commonly used in story conferences than *motivation*. Yet I've discovered that certain professionals are misty about what it means. *Motivation* is the long way of spelling *why*. What urges your character to do something in your story? Why does he do it? That is his motivation.

Words Fail You

There are many kinds of third-act trouble. Beware of that smashing climax when your characters gather to talk out their problems like civilized, sensible folk.

To illustrate in reverse, let's take a magnificent exception, which perhaps proves the rule. That was the last act of *Guess Who's Coming to Dinner?* Spencer Tracy gathered the dinner guests around him, and, in a very long speech, moralized away all their racial conflicts. It worked, but just barely, and only because Tracy was a charismatic genius. A lesser personality could have droned the drama to balmy sleep.

Your third-act climax should not be a verbal summation, but a gut experience. It must *play!* In a social drama, it may be the character conflict coming off the back burner, and boiling all over the stove. In tragedy, it is usually the death scene. In an action story, it may be the shootout, or the physical decision, like the title fight in *Rocky*. In *Casablanca* it was the pain of lovers parting. Remember the slugging match between Anne Bancroft and Shirley MacLaine in *The Turning Point?*

Shock Shlock

A coterie of modern filmmakers revel in the error that a crudely written movie is brilliant just because it shocks people. This substitution of raw sex and violence for quality is the trademark of the untalented artist.

Some of them pretend to be unmasking the bloodlust of the human animal. In fact, they are cynically exploiting the evils they profess to expose. The dimmest aspect of this inversion is that it often results in beefy cash profits.

Gross is gross is gross.

The Rebels

Pioneering in filmmaking is often a disinclination to submit to discipline. Remember what Lenin said (and surely he knew): "You cannot make a successful revolution with anarchists."

Invasion of Privacy

The lives of living persons and their personal privacies are protected by U.S. law. No writer can create for public sale a script, play, article, book, or story using the name or specifically identifiable activities of a living person.

Writers have a certain latitude in dealing with incidents and identities of public figures. A newsman or historian, for example, may write an article or story about the deeds or didos of some headline politician.

But do not write a riotous script about a live madame of a Nevada whorehouse. She will sue, and her lawyers might cost you the condominium. The legal philosophy is that one's name, person, and life story are a species of personal property. A person "owns" the publication and dramatic rights to his or her life.

To be sure, such person may be willing to sell you those rights for a fee, or a percentage of profits. But be sure you sign the deal *before* you write the script. Otherwise you may find yourself in legal possession of 135 pages of nothing.

Living persons, in brief, are live hand grenades. Don't pull the pin on them. Wait until they have been gathered. The dead are in public domain.

Question and Answer

Say you are a student—or an otherwise novice writer—and you could now ask one question. What would it be?

My private poll, based on thousands of questions asked by all my UCLA classes through the years, predicts this one:

"What are the practical working habits of professional writers?"

The best working habit for any writer—male, female, psychopathic, or Peruvian—is whatever gets the script done. Of that pattern, there are endless variations.

A highly professional friend of mine, who writes big novels as well as big movies, has to start before ten in the morning. If he isn't at his desk by that hour, putting down words on paper, he just has to say the hell with it. He goes out to play golf. Or perhaps to his psychiatrist to find out why he isn't working.

But his shrink can't tell him much, except not to worry. *All his* writers have problems working. One brilliant dramatist-patient of his never really gets down to it until after midnight. By then his family is in bed and the house is still. He opens a bottle of vodka and turns wee small hours into big-dollar dream sessions.

But most writers can't write their laundry lists while drinking. Drugs, I am told by reliable addicts, make you feel you are writing Shakespeare's sonnets. But later the stuff may be musky as enchanted garbage.

Of course, it's that getting started in the morning that's the hardest part. Billions of man- and woman-hours have been lost sharpening pencils or long pink fingernails. Ernest Hemingway wrote the best prescription against morning procrastination that I know of.

Hemingway would quit work each day, leaving an incomplete page or passage. Next morning, first thing, he would have to read over what he had written. That is the vanity impulse no writer can resist. When you come to that incomplete bit, you have almost a compulsion to finish it. Putting those first few words on paper gets your juices flowing. Then the normal creative process takes charge, and you're in gear for the day.

The important point is not to bug yourself about any

unorthodox working habits. Different brains and bodies have different rhythms. None of them shows on your final shooting script. But do not depend on your kinks, either. Honor that dumb old cliché about inspiration being mostly perspiration. The fact is that most successful professional writers report to work soon after breakfast and quit around sundown to go home to dinner. Like ditch diggers.

17.

HOLLYWOOD
PILGRIMAGE

Time was when earnest, healthy-minded Americans dreamed of becoming President of the United States. That shining obsession has been replaced by the modern urge to crash television or the motion-picture industry. Campuses and youth groups everywhere are alive with aspiring producers, actors, directors, writers, cinematographers. Brilliant student and apprentice films are made in literally hundreds of training programs. The *Los Angeles Times* reports that ten thousand hopefuls a year pour from schools and colleges with film credits or cinema degrees as high as Ph.D.

Most of the graduate dreamers among them entrain, enplane, enbus, or enjalopy straight for California. The one thing they know for sure about getting a film job is that they're not going to be hired from a résumé dropped in the mail. On arrival in Hollywood, they run into the stark raving reality that there are almost no jobs to be found.

There are, to be sure, grants and studio or craft apprentice programs. The industry is well aware of the onrush of dedicated, intelligent people, and tries its best to do something about it. But less than one qualified applicant in a hundred is lucky enough to snatch one of those rare brass rings. Those are terrible odds. To buck them you need to be compulsive, obsessed, perhaps even a little balmy.

Successful men and women in any art are often compulsive and balmy. People like that don't consider the odds. They just sneak up at night and cut their own holes in the fence.

Two holes in the fence offer practical access to the motion-picture industry. Writing is one of them, and the other is hard cash money. Who are most of those executive producers whose names flash in glowing letters on the screen among the film's main titles? Some few are true professionals, who have earned their command positions. But most of them are money guns, who maneuvered the many millions required to meet that film's furious production costs.

Therefore, if you have a gentle grandmother, endowed with sinful Dun & Bradstreet statistics, bring her with you to Beverly Hills. In no time, you'll have a lawyer, a big agent, and a choice table at the Bistro. Before you know it, you'll be invited to finance a movie. You'll find your name on an office door, and you'll be included in budget conferences. You'll even be allowed to hang around the set. All this with an ease that makes the legend that film jobs are hard to get ridiculous.

But not many have that generous grandmother. This leaves only one method for us common folk to make it in Hollywood. That is by offering something tangible that the industry wants to buy.

You'll discover that what it does not want to buy is eager inexperience. Hollywood has more urgent, talented inexperience than any hiring hall in the world. That's what makes the odds so steep for unproduced producers, directors, and all other hopefuls.

But what the industry does want to buy—nay, must buy for its survival—are original stories and compelling scripts.

Francis Coppola, John Milius, and Paul Schrader are three recently established directors who picked the Hollywood lock with their typewriter keys.

Dropping to practical, less exalted levels, sift through almost any evening of prime-time television. Even Hollywood professionals will see new, unfamiliar names among the writing credits on the dramatic shows. Membership in the Writers Guild numbers upwards of five thousand, and is constantly growing. Almost every one of those five thousand started with no professional movie or TV record.

No writer can even join the Guild until he has proved his ability with a film or TV screen credit. Whatever the job prospects in other areas, Guild records prove that dozens of new writers make the breakthrough every season.

The *Los Angeles Times* article cited above suggested that there is a Catch-22 in this process. The catch, said the *Times*, lies in the new writer's grueling difficulty in finding a producer who will read, or even an agent who will submit, his freshman work.

Getting an agent is far from easy. A practical approach to the problem is outlined in Chapter 14. But easy or difficult, it's far from impossible. Talent agents can't exist without talented clients. In over twenty years of my workshop course at UCLA, dozens of agents, great and small, have asked me to recommend to them promising new people. I have never had one student with valid talents who could not find an agent to peddle his product.

The key, of course, lies in the words *valid talents*. Agents and producers are flooded with the commonplace. Routine work will get you nothing but routine indifference. To crack the hard ice, a new writer must show them something special, extra, and different.

One night at UCLA a couple of years back, this opinion sparked an angry outburst. An attractive, indignant young lady replied, in effect, "The hell with those fancy ideas about being special and different. Who needs all that stuff about quality, and content, and special characters. Why don't you just teach us how to write and sell the goddamn crap we see on the tube every night?"

The answer, of course, was direct and obvious. Agents and producers don't want just added servings of routine junk. They're choked with it already. Our class discussions (and the chapters of this book) are not just a training exercise for enshrined mediocrity.

Most networks, producers, and agents are bitterly aware of the dreariness of such product. A moving drama remains to be written about the schizoid TV producer who can't let his own children watch his weekly series. The fact that much of this commercial product is so grossly ordinary is the single strongest incentive for the beginning writer. Because that gives him or her the clearest chance of any new talent in town to crash the party.

WHO WROTE THE SCRIPT?

Writers' credits for film and TV scripts cited in this book.

The African Queen. Screenplay by James Agee and John Huston. Novel by C. S. Forester

All About Eve. Screenplay by Joseph L. Mankiewicz. Based on story by Mary Orr.

All Quiet on the Western Front. Screenplay by George Abbott, Maxwell Anderson, and Dell Andrews. Novel by Erich Maria Remarque.

All the President's Men. Screenplay by William Goldman. Based on book by Carl Bernstein and Bob Woodward.

American Graffiti. Written by George Lucas, Gloria Katz, and Willard Huyck.

Annie Hall. Written by Woody Allen and Marshall Brickman.

The Apartment. Written by Billy Wilder and I. A. L. Diamond.

The Autobiography of Miss Jane Pittman. Teleplay by Tracy Keenan Wynn. Novel by Ernest J. Gaines.

The Birth of a Nation. Scenario by D. W. Griffith and Frank Woods. Based on novel *The Clansman* by Thomas Dixon.

Bonnie and Clyde. Written by David Newman and Robert Benton.

Boys' Town. Screenplay by Dore Schary and John Meehan. Story by Schary and Eleanore Griffin.

Brian's Song. Teleplay by William Blinn. Based on book by Gale Sayers with Al Silverman. Film also released theatrically.

The Bridge on the River Kwai. Novel by Pierre Boulle. The legend persists that Carl Foreman and Michael Wilson worked on the screenplay with Boulle.

Butch Cassidy and the Sundance Kid. Written by William Goldman.

Butterflies Are Free. Screenplay by Leonard Gershe, from his play.

Cabaret. Screenplay by Jay Presson Allen and Hugh Wheeler. From stage musical by Joe Masteroff (music and lyrics by John Kander and Fred Ebb), play *I Am a Camera* by John Van Druten, and the story "Sally Bowles" in book *Goodbye to Berlin* by Christopher Isherwood.

Camille. Screenplay by Zoë Akins, Frances Marion, and James Hilton. Novel and play by Alexandre Dumas.

Casablanca. Screenplay by Julius J. Epstein, Philip G. Epstein, and Howard Koch. Play by Murray Burnett and Joan Alison.

A Case of Rape. Teleplay by Robert E. Thompson, from story by Louis Rudolph.

The Charlatan. Teleplay by Wells Root, for General Electric Theatre.

A Christmas Story. Teleplay by Truman Capote.

Cimarron. Screenplay by Howard Estabrook. Novel by Edna Ferber.

Citizen Kane. The release print accorded screenplay credit to Herman J. Mankiewicz and Orson Welles. Controversy continues.

Close Encounters of the Third Kind. Written by Steven Spielberg.

The Covered Wagon. Screen adaptation by James Cunningham. Novel by Emerson Hough.

Cyrano de Bergerac. Screenplay by Carl Foreman. Play by Edmond Rostand.

Dark Victory. Screenplay by Casey Robinson. Play by George Brewer, Jr., and Bertram Bloch.

The Day of the Locust. Screenplay by Waldo Salt. Novel by Nathanael West.

Death of a Salesman. Screenplay by Stanley Roberts. Play by Arthur Miller.

Deliverance. Screenplay by James Dickey, from his novel.

Dinner at Eight. Screenplay by Frances Marion and Herman J. Mankiewicz. Added dialogue by Donald Ogden Stewart. From play by George S. Kaufman and Edna Ferber.

Dr. Jekyll and Mr. Hyde. Screenplay by Percy Heath and Samuel Hoffenstein (1932—Frederic March version). Screenplay by John Lee Mahin (1941—Spencer Tracy version). Story by Robert Louis Stevenson.

Doctor Zhivago. Screenplay by Robert Bolt. Novel by Boris Pasternak.

Dog Day Afternoon. Screenplay by Frank Pierson, based on magazine article by P. F. Kluge and Thomas Moore.

Earthquake. Written by George Fox and Mario Puzo.

Easy Rider. Written by Terry Southern, Peter Fonda, and Dennis Hopper.

8½. Screenplay by Federico Fellini, Ennio Flaiano, Brunello Rondi, and Tuilio Pinelli. Story by Fellini and Flaiano.

The Eiger Sanction. Written by Hal Dresner, Warren B. Murphy, and Rod Whitaker.

The Exorcist. Screenplay by William Peter Blatty, from his novel.

Farewell to Manzanar. Teleplay by Jeanne Wakatsuki, James D. Huston, and John Korty.

"The Fire Dancer." Teleplay by Alvin Sargent (episode of TV series "Empire").

Five Easy Pieces. Screenplay by Bob Rafelson and Adrien Joyce. Story by Joyce.

Funny Girl. Screenplay by Isabel Lennart from her musical play (lyrics by Bob Merrill and music by Jule Styne).

Gentleman's Agreement. Screenplay by Moss Hart. Novel by Laura Z. Hobson.

The Glass House. Teleplay by Truman Capote.

The Godfather. Screenplay by Mario Puzo and Francis Ford Coppola, based on Puzo's story.

The Godfather Part II. Screenplay by Francis Ford Coppola and Mario Puzo, based on novel by Puzo.

Gone with the Wind. Screenplay by Sidney Howard. Novel by Margaret Mitchell.

The Goodbye Girl. Written by Neil Simon.

Goodbye, Mr. Chips. Screenplay (1939—Robert Donat version) by R. C. Sheriff, Claudine West, and Eric Maschwitz. Novel by James Hilton.

The Graduate. Screenplay by Calder Willingham and Buck Henry. Novel by Charles Webb.

Guess Who's Coming to Dinner? Written by William Rose.

The Guns of Navarone. Screenplay by Carl Foreman. Novel by Alistair MacLean.

Harry and Tonto. Written by Paul Mazursky and Josh Greenfeld.

Heaven Knows, Mr. Allison. Screenplay by John Lee Mahin and John Huston. Novel by Charles Shaw.

High Noon. Screenplay by Carl Foreman, based on story by John W. Cunningham.

Hiroshima Mon Amour. Written by Marguerite Duras.

The Hospital. Written by Paddy Chayefsky.

The Hunchback of Notre Dame. Scenario by Edward T. Lowe. Screen adaptation by Perry Poore Sheehan. Novel by Victor Hugo.

Hustling. Teleplay by Fay Kanin, based on book by Gail Sheehy.

Icebound. Screenplay by Clara Beranger. Play by Owen Davis.

I Cover the Waterfront. Screenplay by Wells Root. Added dialogue by Jack Jevne. Based on book by Max Miller.

I Never Sang for My Father. Screenplay by Robert Anderson, from his play.

The Informer. Screenplay by Dudley Nichols. Story by Liam
    O'Flaherty.
In the Heat of the Night. Screenplay by Sterling Silliphant,
    based on novel by John Ball.
It Happened One Night. Screenplay by Robert Riskin. Story by
    Samuel Hopkins Adams.
I Want to Live. Written by Nelson Gidding and Don M.
    Mankiewicz.

Jaws. Screenplay by Peter Benchley and Carl Gottlieb. Novel
    by Benchley.
Jaws 2. Screenplay by Carl Gottlieb and Howard Sackler,
    based on characters created by Peter Benchley.
Julia. Screenplay by Alvin Sargent, based on material in Lil-
    lian Hellman's book *Pentimento*.

The King and I. Screenplay by Ernest Lehman, from the novel
    by Margaret Landon, and the stage musical by Oscar
    Hammerstein II and Richard Rodgers.
King Kong. Screenplay by James Creelman and Ruth Rose.
    Story by Meriam C. Cooper and Edgar Wallace. For the
    1976 remake, the screenplay was by Lorenzo Semple, Jr.,
    based on the Creelman-Rose script.
Kiss and Tell. Screenplay by F. Hugh Herbert, from his play.
Kotch. Screenplay by John Paxton. Novel by Katherine
    Topkins.

Lady Sings the Blues. Screenplay by Terence McCloy, Chris
    Clark, and Suzanne de Passe, based on book by Billie
    Holiday.
The Last Picture Show. Screenplay by Larry McMurtry and
    Peter Bogdanovich, based on McMurtry's novel.
Last Year at Marienbad. Screenplay by Alain Robbe-Grillet.
L'Avventura. Written by Michelangelo Antonioni, Elio Bartoli-
    ni, and Tonino Guerra.
Lawrence of Arabia. Screenplay by Robert Bolt. Based on the
    writings of Col. T. E. Lawrence.

Life with Father. Screenplay by Donald Ogden Stewart. Novel by Clarence Day. Play by Howard Lindsay and Russel Crouse.

Little Caesar. Screenplay by Francis Faragoh and Robert N. Lee. Novel by W. R. Burnett.

Little Moon of Alban. Teleplay by James Costigan.

Looking for Mr. Goodbar. Screenplay by Richard Brooks. Novel by Judith Rossner.

The Lost Weekend. Screenplay by Charles Brackett and Billy Wilder. Novel by Charles R. Jackson.

Love Story. Screenplay by Erich Segal, which he later developed into the novel.

Magnificent Obsession. Screenplay (1935 version) by Sarah Y. Mason and Victor Heerman, from novel by Lloyd C. Douglas. 1954 remake—screenplay by Robert Blees. Adaptation by Wells Root, based on the above.

The Magnificent Seven. Screenplay by William Roberts. Based on Japanese film *The Seven Samurai*, by Akira Kurosawa, Shinobu Hashimoto, and Hideo Oguni.

Make Way for Tomorrow. Screenplay by Vina Delmar, based on novel by Josephine Laurence.

A Man and a Woman. Screenplay by Pierre Uytterhoeven and Claude Lelouch. Story by Lelouch.

A Man for All Seasons. Screenplay by Robert Bolt, from his play.

Marty. Teleplay and subsequent screenplay by Paddy Chayefsky.

Mary Poppins. Screenplay by Bill Walsh and Don DaGradi, based on books by P. L. Travers.

*M*A*S*H.* Screenplay by Ring Lardner, Jr. Novel by Richard Hooker.

Midnight Cowboy. Screenplay by Waldo Salt. Novel by James Leo Herlihy.

The Missiles of October. Teleplay by Stanley R. Greenberg.

The Moon Is Blue. Screenplay by F. Hugh Herbert, from his play.

Mutiny on the Bounty. Screenplay for the 1935 version by Jules Furthman, Talbot Jennings, and Carey Wilson. Screenplay for the 1962 remake by Charles Lederer. Novel by Charles Nordhoff and James Hall.

My Fair Lady. Screenplay by Alan Lerner. From musical play by Lerner (book and lyrics) and Frederick Loewe (music). All based on George Bernard Shaw's play *Pygmalion.*

My Sweet Charlie Teleplay (later released in theaters) by Richard Levinson and William Link, based on play by David Westheimer.

Network. Written by Paddy Chayefsky.

1984. Screenplay by William P. Templeton and Ralph Bettison Novel by George Orwell.

Of Mice and Men. Screenplay by Gene Solow. Novel by John Steinbeck. Play by George S. Kaufman.

One Flew over the Cuckoo's Nest. Screenplay by Lawrence Hauben and Bo Goldman. Novel by Ken Kesey. Play by Dale Wasserman.

On the Waterfront. Screenplay by Budd Schulberg, based on newspaper articles by Malcolm Johnson.

The Owl and the Pussycat. Screenplay by Buck Henry. Play by Bill Manhoff.

A Patch of Blue. Screenplay by Guy Green, based on story by Elizabeth Kath.

Peter Pan. Screenplay (Disney version) by Ted Sears, Bill Peet, Joe Rinaldi, Erdman Penner, Winston Hibler, Milt Banta, and Ralph Wright. Play by Sir James M. Barrie.

Peyton Place. Screenplay by John Michael Hayes. Novel by Grace Metalious. TV credits multiplex.

Play It Again, Sam. Screenplay by Woody Allen, from his play.

The Poseidon Adventure. Screenplay by Sterling Silliphant. Novel by Paul Gallico.

Pretty Baby. Written by Polly Platt.

The Prisoner of Zenda. Screenplay (1937—Ronald Colman version) by John L. Balderston. Adaptation by Wells Root. Novel by Anthony Hope.

Pygmalion. Screenplay by Leo Dalrymple, Cecil Lewis, and W. P. Lipscomb. Play by George Bernard Shaw.

Rain. Screen adaptation by Maxwell Anderson. Play by John Colton and Clemence Randolph, adapted from story by W. Somerset Maugham.

Rebecca. Screenplay by Robert E. Sherwood and Joan Harrison. Novel by Daphne du Maurier.

Rocky. Written by Sylvester Stallone.

Romeo and Juliet. Screenplay (1968 version) by Franco Brasati and Masolino D'amico. Play by William Shakespeare.

Rosemary's Baby. Screenplay by Roman Polanski. Novel by Ira Levin.

"Roots." Television mini-series developed by William Blinn from book by Alex Haley. Teleplays for various episodes by Blinn, Ernest Kinoy, and Charles Cohen.

Ruggles of Red Gap. Screenplay by Walter de Leon and Harlan Thompson. Adaptation by Humphrey Pearson. Novel by Harry Leon Wilson.

Saturday Night Fever. Screenplay by Norman Wexler, based on story by Nik Cohn.

Scent of a Woman. Screenplay by Ruggero Maccari and Dino Risi. Novel by Giovanni Arpino.

Scared Straight. Television fictional-documentary by Arnold Shapiro.

Serpico. Screenplay by Waldo Salt and Norman Wexler, based on book by Peter Maas.

Seventh Heaven. Screenplay by Benjamin Glazer. Stage play and film adaptation by Austin Strong.

Shampoo. Written by Robert Towne and Warren Beatty.

Sounder. Screenplay by Lonnie Elder 3rd. Novel by William H. Armstrong.

The Sound of Music. Screenplay by Ernest Lehman. Stage musical book by Howard Lindsay and Russel Crouse, suggested by Maria Augusta Trapp's story. (Music by Richard Rodgers and lyrics by Oscar Hammerstein II.)

The Spy Who Came in from the Cold. Screenplay by Paul Dehn and Guy Trosper, from novel by John LeCarre.

The Spy Who Loved Me. Screenplay by Christopher Wood and Richard Maibaum.

Stagecoach. Screenplay by Dudley Nichols, based on story by Ernest Haycox.

Star Wars. Written by George Lucas.

State of the Union. Screenplay by Anthony Veiller and Myles Connolly. Play by Howard Lindsay and Russel Crouse.

The Sting. Written by David S. Ward.

The Story of Louis Pasteur. Written by Pierre Collings and Sheridan Gibney.

A Streetcar Named Desire. Screenplay by Tennessee Williams, from adaptation by Oscar Saul. Play by Williams.

Superman. Screenplay by Mario Puzo, David Newman, Leslie Newman, Robert Benton. Story by Puzo.

A Tale of Two Cities. Screenplay (1935—Ronald Colman version) by W. P. Lipscomb and S. N. Behrman. Novel by Charles Dickens.

A Taste of Honey. Screenplay by Shelagh Delaney and Tony Richardson. Play by Delaney.

Taxi Driver. Written by Paul Schrader.

Texas Across the River. Written by Wells Root, Harold Greene, and Ben Starr.

Tiger Shark. Screenplay by Wells Root, from story by Houston Branch.

The Towering Inferno. Screenplay by Sterling Silliphant, based on novels by Richard Martin Stern, and by Thomas N. Scortia and Frank M. Robinson.

Treasure Island. Screenplay by John Lee Mahin. Story by Robert Louis Stevenson.

The Treasure of the Sierra Madre. Screenplay by John Huston Novel by B. Traven.

True Grit. Screenplay by Marguerite Roberts. Novel by Charles Portis.

The Turning Point. Written by Arthur Laurents.

Two for the Road. Written by Frederic Raphael.

2001: A Space Odyssey. Written by Stanley Kubrick and Arthur C. Clark

The Unholy Three. (1923 version.) Adaptation by Todd Browning, from a story by C. A. Robbins.

An Unmarried Woman. Written by Paul Mazursky.

The Virginian. Screenplay by Frances Goodrich and Albert Hackett. Novel by Owen Wister.

The Virgin Spring (Swedish title *Jungfraukallan*). Screenplay by Ulla Isaksson, based on fourteenth-century ballad.

West Side Story. Screenplay by Ernest Lehman. From stage musical by Arthur Laurents (music by Leonard Bernstein and lyrics by Stephen Sondheim).

Who's Afraid of Virginia Woolf? Screenplay by Ernest Lehman. Play by Edward Albee.

AUTHOR'S CREDENTIALS

Wells Root began his professional writing career in the 1920s as a reporter in New York for the legendary *World*. He moonlighted doing film and dramatic criticism for *Time*, and later became an associate editor of that newsmagazine.

When talking pictures began, Paramount Pictures brought him to California on contract. Since then he has written stories, adaptations, or screenplays for major films such as *I Cover the Waterfront*, *The Prisoner of Zenda* (Selznick version), *Bird of Paradise*, *Tiger Shark*, *Magnificent Obsession*, *Texas Across the River*, and some two dozen others.

He has also written fiction and fact pieces for various magazines. He is a founder-member of The Writers Guild of America, West. In 1940 a comedy called *As You Are*, on which Root and Hugh Mills collaborated, opened at London's Aldwych Theatre. After cordial reviews and ninety-eight prosperous performances, it closed suddenly. The German Luftwaffe bombed out the theater.

In television, Root has written over seventy scripts for various series such as "The General Electric Theatre," "Fireside Theatre," "Ford Theatre," "Four Star Playhouse," "Maverick," "Cheyenne," and "The Rogues "

In the 1950s he was asked to teach a course in film and TV writing technique at UCLA Extension. He has been doing so ever since. He has come to believe that other professional writers would do well to gather novices around them and try to explain their elusive craft. Many will discover, as he did, that only by teaching it can they learn what the hell they've been doing.

INDEX